GATT and Conf... ...gement

Published in cooperation with the
Peace Research Institute Frankfurt,
Federal Republic of Germany

GATT and Conflict Management

A Transatlantic Strategy
for a Stronger Regime

EDITED BY

Reinhard Rode

Westview Press

BOULDER • SAN FRANCISCO • OXFORD

Published in 1990 in the United States of America by Westview Press, Inc., 5500 Central Avenue, Boulder, Colorado 80301, and in the United Kingdom by Westview Press, 36 Lonsdale Road, Summertown, Oxford OX2 7EW

Library of Congress Cataloging-in-Publication Data
GATT and conflict management: a transatlantic strategy for a stronger
  regime/edited by Reinhard Rode.
    p. cm.
  ISBN 0-8133-7967-9
  1. General Agreement on Tariffs and Trade (Organization).
2. Conflict management. I. Rode, Reinhard, 1947–   .
HF1721.G35 1990
382'.92—dc20   90-12498
                                                                CIP

Printed and bound in the United States of America

  The paper used in this publication meets the requirements
(∞) of the American National Standard for Permanence of Paper
  for Printed Library Materials Z39.48-1984.

10   9   8   7   6   5   4   3   2   1

Contents

Preface

This volume grew out of an October 1988 conference on GATT issues held at the Peace Research Institute Frankfurt (PRIF), Federal Republic of Germany. The lively debate at this international meeting is reflected in the articles published in this volume. The conclusions of the editor, particularly his strong recommendation for a new transatlantic leadership effort for the GATT, are his own responsibility and are not the outcome of a consensus among the contributors.

The editor is grateful to the Volkswagen Foundation for having granted funds for the conference and the John D. and Catherine T. MacArthur Foundation for its support for the publication. We would like to thank the staff at Westview Press for their help in moving the project forward on their publishing schedule.

Reinhard Rode

1

Introduction

Reinhard Rode

The 1960s, and to a lesser degree the 1970s, were generally perceived as a successful period for the General Agreement on Tariffs and Trade (GATT). There is no question that it greatly contributed to the expansion of world trade and hence to peace and prosperity. Not only did it help intra-Western trade recover and stabilize but, by refraining from injecting too high a dose of politics into trade conflicts, it had a favorable impact on the Atlantic alliance, too. As for the 1980s, they have turned out to be a frustrating decade for GATT. Trade questions have become heavily politicized and have generated new and severe conflicts. After tremendous initial progress in tariff reductions, the GATT momentum has slowed down dramatically as the new non-tariff barriers, or NTBs, are proving very difficult to eliminate. But since they are of an extremely complex nature, it can be argued that GATT is a victim of its own earlier success. NTBs are deeply rooted in the domestic structures of the respective contracting parties, thus bringing into stark relief the tensions that arise when international cooperation supplants national interests, i.e., once independent nations have to relinquish some of their sovereignty in economic matters. But since this is a widespread phenomenon, GATT does not stand alone. Compared with the IMF, however, it may suffer more because of its limited character as an international agreement.

The limits of GATT, a remnant of what had been envisioned as something called the International Trade Organization (whose charter was never ratified by the U.S. Congress), were less obvious as long as U.S. leadership remained strong. Looking back, one can say that by and large the period of U.S. hegemony benefited the GATT. American pressure for free trade became weaker the more the United States turned out to be a relative loser in the wake of trade liberalization. The huge trade deficits of the United States in the 1980s bear witness to this. American national trade interests and liberal trade principles no longer automatically

1

coincide. U.S. trade policy has changed. GATT and its logical corollary of multilateral liberalizing trade activities have lost momentum and have become but one strategy—if still the major one—along with two others, unilateral trade nationalism and bilateralism (reciprocity), which are on the rise. No one can be certain at this stage that multilateralism will maintain its position as the number one U.S. trade strategy. Jeffrey Schott addresses this in Chapter 3.

Declining American leadership in GATT, the U.S.-initiated current Uruguay Round notwithstanding, focused attention on the hegemonic stability theory. American scholars like Steven Krasner and Robert Gilpin argue that a system like GATT needs a hegemon, or leader, to guarantee stable cooperation. The Europeans, and probably the Japanese as well, dislike this perspective, perceiving it as a claim for U.S. neohegemony. Institutionalists such as Robert Keohane offer a more sanguine alternative: stable cooperation after hegemony. *After Hegemony* also happens to be the title of a book by Mr. Keohane.

The basic assumption is that a regime like GATT—with its principle, norms, rules and decision-making procedures—is viable and can prevail without a leader. The advantages flowing from a GATT reorganized along these lines would benefit all participants; they would also help stabilize the system, if only because the sole alternative would be complete trade anarchy, an orgy of bilateralism. And GATT, so the idea, has an embedded strength: it lies in its being able to last only as a *multilateral* trade agreement. The open question, however, is whether GATT will be capable of developing further and of initiating new liberalization efforts by itself. To be sure, the GATT bureaucracy could do it—the paperwork it generates in terms of proposals is impressive enough. But would such bureaucratic politics prove sufficient? I, for one, doubt it. What I think we need are new initiators of regime development to pursue trade liberalization efforts, to assist the weakened former leader and pick up the flag of the free trade ideal, i.e., GATT's free trade principle.

Who else but the European Community and Japan could perform this task? Unfortunately, neither has volunteered so far. The European Community has turned sharply inward, seemingly preoccupied with the overriding idea of bringing about its single market. Outsiders fear the emergence of a "Fortress Europe." As for Japan, it just keeps on smiling and relentlessly goes on exporting (while importing only reluctantly) and thus does not seem ready to assume the role of promoter of liberal trade practices. Since neither the United States nor the European Community nor Japan seem ready, willing or capable to take up that role individually, why don't they assume it jointly? For quite some time, the Trilateral Commission fostered the idea of such a triumvirate to steer

GATT around the treacherous shoals of bilateralism toward the more rewarding shores of multilateralism. But the enthusiasm generated during the meetings of this trilateral elite was never contagious enough to sway the governments of the three trading blocs, which seemed intent on pursuing their bilateral quarrels within GATT and, in my view, even more so outside of it. Such behavior was not made to inject any new strength into the flagging GATT regime; it only precipitated its neglect.

There exist no other potential initiators. Newly industrializing countries, or NICs, behave in a development-oriented way, stressing the infant-industry argument for trade. They are not strong enough and their narrow national trade interests put them at odds with the principle of free trade. As to poor countries, they ask for more preferential treatment and are divorced from the liberal trade principle. Some countries with centrally planned economies would like to subscribe to the GATT. The Soviet Union, for example, is about to join it. But such countries are small traders par excellence and do not share the liberal trade ideal at all. Most likely, their rationale for seeking participation in GATT's affairs is to obtain some sort of preferential treatment, too. Of course, their socialist pride does not allow them to say so openly. More influence for any of these groups might push GATT in the direction of UNCTAD, making it like the latter a forum for Third World demands, not for a liberal trade order. Thus one major problem GATT may face is that of an "overload," inevitable result of its global aspirations. I would put it this way: the global integration function suffers when the attractiveness of the liberal trade principle fades, and the attractiveness of this principle fades if the large traders cease to act as role models.

Pressure on the liberal trade principle has come not only from developing countries and from those with centrally planned economies, which do not adhere to this principle, but increasingly, too, from the large traders with their tradition of liberal trading practices. The United States has already been mentioned; as for the European Community, its upcoming single market is clearly aimed at achieving regional goals at the expense of global liberal trade principles. The third player and world export champion, Japan, has not actually converted to trade liberalism and has proven very slow in altering its highly successful export-oriented growth strategy. This may undermine the principle of liberal trade in a dual way. First, Japan's economic decision makers will not use the liberal trade philosophy as their guide, for they merely pay occasional lip service to trade liberalism, more, I think, as a consequence of external pressure and expectations than of changing convictions—Hiroshi Kitamura expounds on this in Chapter 4. Second, the Japanese example of success by means of an explicitly restrictive trade strategy based on economic nationalism was instrumental in causing the economic elites of other countries to question their longstanding belief in the liberal trade principle. Thus my fear that this principle has entered a period of heavy turbulence, fraught with grave danger, as the most successful trader remains seemingly reluctant to subscribe to it.

A structural change in protectionism also places additional stress on the liberal trade principle. The former pattern was more or less to place agriculture and declining industries under a national protectionist wing and to permit relatively free trade for the modern industrial sector, based on the motto "The more advanced products and technologies, the freer their trade." Competing industrial policies and a general trend to ward high-tech protectionism may change this. World trade is likely to become less free, as the dual pressures of traditional and high-tech protectionism grow heavier. This trend toward changing the rules of the game, i.e., making organized trade the rule and free trade the exception, bodes ill for the future of the latter.

These dark clouds gathering over the horizon of free trade demonstrate how vital it is to inject new strength into the liberal trade principle, as the sine qua non for a revival of the GATT regime. With the United States, GATT's former undisputed leader, turning out to be a loser at the game of free trade, the European Community turning increasingly inward, and Japan proving slow to adapt to the liberal trade principle, it can definitely be said that the regime is in deep trouble. While it will no doubt survive for lack of any credible alternatives, it can be expected to sink gradually into relative irrelevance. The views of a Colbert, List or Kitamura rather than those of a Smith or Ricardo would then be its lowest common denominator.

Thus GATT might just evolve into a mere bargaining platform for the organization of world trade, assuming the role of a broker for "orderly marketing agreements." The only real alternative I can foresee is that of a continuing institutional belief in the prevailing regime, coupled with the hope that a liberal trilateral or bilateral transatlantic leadership will eventually come to pass. This optimistic scenario posits that the three (or at least two) giant trade partners constitute more than the mere sum of egocentric actors, that they play a positive leadership role collectively. The ability to play a responsible global role and to overcome narrow national interests finds strong backing in fairly recent history. The beggar-thy-neighbor policies of the 1930s and their economically and politically catastrophic consequences are a case in point and should act as a powerful deterrent. But how long this consensual transatlantic interpretation of the past will last (and how strong its global impact will be) remains to be seen.

The concept of the GATT regime and of a trilateral (or bilateral) leadership of liberal traders reinforcing each other is a highly optimistic vision. A trilateral or bilateral transatlantic management, which would use the GATT framework as a means of promoting the common Western liberal trade principle, would certainly appear to constitute a desirable and reasonable alternative. But it is not at all self-evident or automatic. Whether a responsible joint leadership takes over very soon, or only after some future economic disaster brought about by competing mercantilisms has given the necessary impetus, therefore, is a question that should provide trade analysts with a fascinating field of study for the rest of the millennium. A comparative perspective for the GATT regime, by means of policy analyses for various countries by scholars and experts from different disciplines (economics, political science and international law) and with a practical background, may help develop prospects and strategies for strengthening a regime which most of us consider worth encouraging to prevail and function as efficiently as possible.

2

The GATT Regime:
Issues and Prospects

Gerard Curzon and Victoria Curzon Price

The Uruguay Round of trade negotiations, launched at Punta del Este, Uruguay, in September 1986, underwent a midterm review in Montreal, Canada, in December 1988. The tough period still lies ahead. People who take an interest in these matters are either academic observers or practicing diplomats. For the former, the issues appear to be simple, for the latter, they are of an unbelievable complexity, requiring for their solution all the subtle skills of their trade: pragmatism, reasonable behavior, compromise.

It is clear to which camp we belong. And within that camp, we are not among those who believe that the exceptions to the GATT system should be condoned on grounds of expediency. The international trade system may be in crisis, GATT may be honored more in the breach than in the observance, but it is essential to bear in mind what constitutes a viable international trade order. The principles upon which a "good" international trade system should be run are not even very difficult to live up to: more trade is usually better than less trade, multilateralism is to be preferred to bilateralism, the balance of trade should be a matter of macroeconomic management, not of trade policy. There is not much more to it than that. In fact, if countries could live up to just one principle, the one enshrined in GATT's Article I—the most-favored-nation clause—then we would have no preferential arrangements, no Multifibre Arrangement, no Voluntary Export Restraints (VERs), no Orderly Marketing Arrangements (OMAs), no bilateral semi-conductor agreement between the United States and Japan—in fact, none of the exciting things that the international trade system offers us for analysis.

Clearly, the academic view of the world trade system as it should be differs quite dramatically from the world trade system as it actually is.

This raises the interesting question of why governments pay lip service to GATT and freer trade, but often end up acting differently—a worthy subject of analysis in itself, which has found an intellectually satisfactory answer in the theory of public choice.

And it is because we now understand why democracies, via the lobbying process, generate a certain "supply" of protection to respond to constant demands for it, that we have to approach the future of the GATT system with our eyes open. It is no longer enough to exhort countries to conduct themselves better and explain the merits of non-discriminatory trade, open markets and competition. We have to imagine ways of building a political constituency for freer trade and we have to examine the use of power to achieve this objective.

This chapter will present what I consider to be a series of potential dangers and obstacles on the road to a successful conclusion of the Uruguay Round. It makes no attempt to be comprehensive, for the important and potentially lethal (for the Uruguay Round) issue of agriculture will not be discussed. The material is organized under three headings: the changing attitude of the United States toward the GATT; the implications of the post-1992 single European market for GATT and the Uruguay Round; and the future of multilateralism.

Changing Attitude of the United States to the Multilateral Trade System

Section 301 Investigations

Until the early 1980s GATT was the principal vehicle through which the United States conducted its trade policy. It initiated all the "GATT Rounds," made sure that the European Economic Community gave it, and others, proper compensation for the use of Article XXIV, and generally supported the universal, multilateral philosophy behind the Treaty, which it had largely inspired and brought into being in 1947. In particular, the United States was content with making sure that the EC and Japan played an active part in the various rounds, and let large numbers of developing countries, and some small developed countries, enjoy relatively free access to the U.S. market without asking for or obtaining any dismantling of protection on their part.

This rather lofty attitude has changed. The United States now wants to have access to other countries' markets on the same terms as it offers to imports coming into the United States. This is known as "fair" trade and has involved the United States in a large number of arm-twisting bilateral negotiations with a long list of countries, based on Section 301 of the 1974 Trade Act. This, as is well known, provides for the introduction of unilateral measures by the United States against other countries' unfair trade practices. Since 1985 the threat of such sanctions has been used 26 times by the Reagan administration to try to extract trade concessions from ten different trade partners on a bilateral and unrequited basis. Only three times did the United States actually introduce sanctions: unilateral concessions were obtained in most cases.

These negotiations may have had a positive effect on the multilateral trade system, insofar as the United States uses its powers of persuasion to open up previously closed markets *multilaterally*. However, there are many dangers to the multilateral trade system in these strong-arm tactics. It goes too much against the grain, politically, for countries which are singled out for threatened Section 301 retaliation to offer the whole world the concessions extracted by the United States. They will do all they can to find concessions not covered by GATT, or inherently ambiguous, for instance in the field of non-tariff barriers, in order to target their change of policy at the United States alone. And in any case, the legality of the U.S. sanctions themselves, in the event of the negotiations being unsuccessful, is extremely doubtful.

For instance, as a result of a U.S.-initiated 301 negotiation, Japan agreed to liberalize its cigarette imports in 1986. The purpose was to improve access to the large and very lucrative Japanese market for U.S.-type cigarettes. The Japanese tariff concession was certainly on an *erga omnes* basis, but further promises to ease the certification and distribution procedure would be possible to target in a discriminatory manner in favour of the U.S. After all, one can see why Japan would make every effort to reduce the scope of the concession to prevent EC cigarette producers from getting a "free ride" out of it. Especially as the United States, under 301 negotiations, offers no concessions, just the promise not to introduce retaliatory trade measures against the "unfair" trade practice; and of course, the EC offers no concessions either.

The "tin-opener" effect of 301 actions (and now "Super 301" actions under the new trade legislation) is bound to have an effect on the international trade system, one way or the other. Either, on balance, it pries open previously highly protected foreign markets (like Korea's, or Taiwan's) so that the "free riders" during previous GATT Rounds are willy nilly dragged into the multilateral trade system, or it fosters a worrying sort of bilateralism. For instance, Korea in 1985 unilaterally reduced its barriers on importing and distributing U.S. motion pictures and TV programs, in order to avoid retaliatory action on its exports of TVs and videos to the United States. Was this concession made available to the rest of the world in conformity with GATT's Article IV? In March 1988 Japan agreed to permit U.S. companies to bid (with some hope of not being discriminated against) for major Japanese construction projects.

Are EC companies offered the same advantages? Or for that matter, do Japanese contractors enjoy the same privileges in U.S. or EC markets? The Nippon Telegraph and Telephone Company has for some time promised U.S. products nondiscriminatory treatment in its purchasing policies. I am pretty sure that European firms do not have similar rights. Why should they? European PTTs have surely not offered Japanese or American firms equal rights to bid. They are only just thinking about extending such rights to other Community firms.

In short, when Section 301 is used to open markets in goods which are covered by GATT, there is a fair chance that the concession will be multilateral, at least in name. But where Section 301 is used in areas which are not covered by GATT, then there is no reason to suppose that the concessions are made on any other than a bilateral and discriminatory basis. Finally, there is no doubt at all that sanctions, if and when imposed, are carefully targeted to hit the offending country and it alone. During the dispute over the accession of Spain and Portugal to the European Community, for example, the United States announced it would impose quotas on EC agricultural products but did not carry out this threat. We leave the detailed discussion of where Super 301 investigations are going to take us to Jeffrey Schott in Chapter 3, but would emphasize that this "Ramboesque" use of power has not gone unnoticed in the European Community, which will doubtless be tempted to introduce similar negotiating powers for itself.

The fact of the matter is that bilateral arm-twisting by a superpower is very effective. Disputes are settled in record time, to the satisfaction of the stronger of the two contestants—compare this with the GATT dispute-settlement procedure, which takes months or years to meander its way to a balanced compromise. Furthermore, to the extent that one of the functions of periodic GATT Rounds is to settle a number of long-standing trade disputes in the context of a "mutually advantageous" global package, the fact that such disputes are now expeditiously settled to the satisfaction of the principal initiator of GATT Rounds means that the Uruguay Round, for instance, will lose part of its substance and function.

It has always been a source of wonder that the United States should uphold the rule of law as the preferred method of achieving its trade policy objectives, in preference to using naked power. So surprise should perhaps be reserved for the fact that the GATT system has lasted as long as it has. U.S. power can be used to good or bad effect, but that is not the point. The point is that the trade *system* is being changed from one based on law to one based on power. This cannot bode well for the future.

The U.S. Trade Deficit

The U.S. trade deficit is in good measure to blame for this state of affairs. Most, perhaps all, economists would maintain that trade deficits have much more to do with macroeconomic policies than with trade policies. But most people are not economists, and most people in the United States believe that their country's deficit is due to Uncle Sam's past generosity in offering such free access to the U.S. market, while other countries have offered nothing in return—hence the broad support, especially in Congress, for Section 301 measures.

It follows that as long as the U.S. trade deficit continues, it is fairly unrealistic to expect the United States to make any major offers in the context of the Uruguay Round. In fact, the public choice approach to trade policy suggests that the United States would be incapable of making many such offers: there are just too many import-sensitive sectors to be accommodated, and the export-sensitive sectors, which would normally be lining up in favor of a big step in the direction of freer trade, are being neutralized with the success of the bilateral Section 301 policy.

Although the depreciation of the U.S. dollar since February 1985 must have helped to build a somewhat larger political constituency for freer trade among U.S. exporters, the U.S. administration has responded to these pressures by developing the bilateral Section 301 route described above, instead of transforming them into requests in the Uruguay Round. This has the unfortunate effect of giving American exporters the impression that their trade objectives can be met at no domestic political cost whatsoever, and drains the Uruguay Round of what little political support it might have commanded.

In the meantime, the Uruguay Round is bound to be seen (and sold to the U.S. Congress and public) as a means of correcting the deficit. It is seen as a way to open up other countries' markets, not U.S. markets, which are quite open enough as it is—look at the deficit, which is caused by other countries' unfair trade policies and our excessive generosity in the past.

Unfortunately, however, GATT Rounds do not operate like 301 investigations. They are based on reciprocity and if the United States puts few offers on the table it will obtain relatively few concessions in return. One must hope that the U.S. trade deficit will be corrected soon enough to save the Uruguay Round.

Regionalism

Many people have already commented on the fact that the United States has abandoned its traditional policy of supporting the universal GATT system and tolerating occasional departures of *other* countries wishing to establish regional free trade areas or customs unions under Article XXIV of GATT. Not many of us would ever have thought, back in the 1960s and 1970s that the United States would itself become a proponent of regional discrimination.

Yet so great has become the frustration of the United States with the perceived inequities of GATT that it has launched a series of bilateral free trade initiatives, the most important and most recent being the U.S.-Canadian free trade agreement. The question is not whether the U.S.-Israeli, the U.S.-Caribbean, the U.S.-Mexican and perhaps even the U.S.-Japanese agreements are—or will be—in conformity with Article XXIV of GATT. One may be pretty sure they will be, at least on paper. The problem is, if the United States can achieve 90 percent of its trade-policy objectives with a combination of Section 301 investigations and bilateral free trade agreements, there will be precious little left for GATT and the Uruguay Round to do, except perhaps negotiate on a bilateral basis with the European Community.

Implications of the Single European Market
for the Uruguay Round

As luck would have it, the twelve members of the European Community have chosen exactly this moment in time to make a major effort to eliminate their internal frontiers and to create a genuine "single market" among themselves. The timing could not be worse. The EC will have its hands full trying to meet its ambitious objective. It will certainly not welcome initiatives from outsiders which might either distract it from its goal or complicate its achievement.

The Single Market concept goes well beyond GATT—in other words, Article XXIV disciplines only apply to a small part of what is happening in Europe. Much of the rest—in services, in establishment, in mutual recognition of norms, standards and technical specifications, in capital movements, in financial services—is uncharted territory as far as international law is concerned. Yet we know that the one thing the Uruguay Round is supposed to do is to get beyond the traditional GATT rules, introduce services into the international trade system and cope with nontariff barriers. This puts the Uruguay Round and the Single Market on a collision course. The EC will be extremely reluctant to tie its hands internationally before it has settled its own internal regime in these matters. This puts the end of the Uruguay Round sometime in the middle of the next decade—about the time when one can expect the U.S. trade deficit to disappear, but possible too late to save the GATT from the ignominy of failure to produce results quickly and efficiently.

Fortress Europe?

For the rest of the world, 1992 represents a threat. No matter how earnestly the EC commissioner for external affairs, Willy de Clercq, tries to reassure audiences the world over that the Single Market is not intended to result in more protectionism vis-à-vis nonmember countries, nobody believes him. Yet on paper the reassurances are there. For example: "The removal of all internal barriers will make the Community more—not less—accessible. Once a product has crossed our external border it will be able to circulate freely throughout the 12 member states."[1] Or again, "Our approach will remain the same as before: to use our growing influence to ensure that the liberalization process which we are pursuing in the Community is accompanied by increasing liberalisation of world markets."[2] Or finally, "The internal market should not close in on itself. In conformity with the provisions of GATT, the Community should be open to third countries, and must negotiate with those countries where necessary to ensure access to their markets for Community exports. It will seek to preserve the balance of advantages accorded, while respecting the identity of the internal market of the Community."[3]

The reason these pronouncements cut no ice is that the Community does not enjoy a particularly good reputation as a free trading, open economy. This may come as a surprise to some commissioners who end up believing their own propaganda, but is in fact the result of too many instances of *ad hoc* protection being introduced whenever free-ish trade has hurt local producers.

Let us look at some of these instances of protectionism by the Community or its members. The "Poitiers" incident has become notorious and will take a long time to live down. Just before Christmas 1985, the French government insisted that all imported video recorders should clear customs at a single, small and unequipped customs post in Poitiers, a city in west central France. This blatant nontariff barrier, a thoroughly illegal measure, led to a radical reduction in the number of video recorders entering the country, but the publicity surrounding the affair was too much to bear, and the measure was quietly withdrawn—after Christmas, naturally. This incident left the feeling that France considered protectionism to be a natural sovereign right of government, a feeling that was not tempered by the existence of the well-known unilateral, informal quotas on the import of Japanese automobiles, by General de Gaulle's personal choice of the SECAM color TV system (incompatible with the more widely used U.S.-based PAL system) and by unilateral quotas imposed on cheap clothing from developing countries.

Nor has France been unique. Britain has also negotiated a so-called "Orderly Marketing Agreement," or OMA, with Japanese carmakers, under which the latter have agreed to limit their car exports to 10 percent of the U.K. market and to "respect" U.K. prices. As for Spain and Portugal, they have imposed a virtual embargo on the import of Japanese cars. All these countries, plus the other members of the European Community, have either actively promoted or have passively accepted the regulation of textile and clothing trade under the aegis of the Multifibre Arrangement. According to a recent Japanese complaint, 11 EC members operate between them 131 nationally imposed quotas on 107 products.[4] Some of these must be "grandfather" quotas going back to 1955, when Japan originally acceded to GATT, but those on fork-lift trucks and TVs must be of a later vintage.

The list of OMAs and VERs (Voluntary Export Restraints) is thought to be long but it is not particularly well documented. OMAs and VERs are the protectionist half-life that prolongs the effect of anti-dumping investigations long after the initial explosion. A great many anti-dumping investigations are brought to an end once the exporting country promises to raise prices and/or restrict exports.[5] Given that the determination of dumping is impossible from an economic point of view,[6] the automatic conclusion is that price undertakings offered by exporting countries are just cartels in the making.

In the 1960s, European countries accepted price undertakings from Japan in labor-intensive, low-tech products like stainless steel flat ware, ceramics, sewing machines, cigarette lighters, fishing tackle, bicycles, clothing, leather goods and so forth. In the 1970s, somewhat more sophisticated goods were "brought under surveillance"—quartz crystal units, acrylic fibres, saccarin, stereo cassette tape heads and steel ball bearings. Finally, in the 1980s, the Community was in the business of restricting imports from Japan (and by this time Taiwan, Korea and others as well) in the field of motor vehicles, numerically-controlled machine tools, color TVs, cathode-ray tubes, light commercial vehicles, motorcyles, quartz watches, hi-fi equipment, fork-lift trucks, videotape recorders, electronic typewriters and microwave ovens.[7]

Now it may be argued that all this is entirely legal and not necessarily cumulative, which may well be true. But anti-dumping duties and price undertakings are ambiguous and the overall impression is that Europeans just do not like competition very much and are well armed to resist it. And one also has the feeling that when dumping cannot be proved, price undertakings are extracted anyway, under threat of the use of GATT's Article XIX,[8] resulting in the proliferation of so-called "gray-area" measures.

This use of power, in flagrant violation of GATT principles (even if rules are not explicitly broken), is of relatively long standing, and shows that the trade order has been gradually shifting from a rule-based to a power-based order for some time.

The main worry for outsiders is that 1992 implies a consolidation of all these restrictions at Community level, which presumably is why Japan has, after all these years, decided to raise the question of quotas in GATT. Not only is the Community consolidating, but it has grown. And there are three new members whose free trade credentials are not of the best. While the free traders in the Community may just muster a blocking minority, they are definitely not in a majority. And do they feel strongly enough about freer trade to resist their partners' pressures? In the past, if a single country, i.e., France, really wanted the Community to introduce Community-wide import restrictions, the others would acquiesce.

So fear of "Fortress Europe" stems in part from the Community's (or its members') past behavior and the fear that the sheer size of the new unit will extract even more "price undertakings" ever more easily.

Another question which worries outsiders is whether European subsidiaries of multinational firms with headquarters outside the EC will be treated fairly. It is all very well for the Commission to cite Article 58 of the Treaty of Rome,[9] which guarantees the right of legally constituted firms to equal treatment. The case of the Nissan Bluebird, which France refuses to treat as "European" although it is made in Wales and has substantial local value-added content, is exactly what outsiders are worried about. It shows that when protectionist sentiment is at issue, the law appears to carry no weight whatsoever. It also shows that the old protectionist reflexes are right there, in very good shape. But pity the poor outsider, for the case raises a great many unanswered questions: How "European" do you have to be? Is it a matter of value-added, as the Nissan case seems to suggest? If so, can we please see the legal text? If the Nissan Bluebird is Japanese, is Airbus not American?

The Nissan case shows that protection can take many forms, including that of treating foreign firms in a discriminatory manner. The trouble is that GATT is silent on this question and that despite half a century of explosive growth in the activities of multinational firms, there is no agreed international code on how governments should behave.

And it is not just protectionism in goods which is at stake, but the entire services area as well. Behind the Nissan Bluebird case lies the question of whether the European subsidiaries of U.S., Japanese, Swiss and other banks, insurance companies, data processing houses, management consultants, lawyers, accountants and so forth will have access to the Single Market on the same terms as their European Community competitors. Will they be treated on an equal footing when it comes to participating in the EC's various programs to promote this or that technology (RACE, BRITE, ESPRIT, etc.) or in the ambitious "EUREKA" program, originally designed to counter former President Ronald Reagan's Strategic Defense Initiative (SDI)? Will European subsidiaries of American, Japanese or Swedish firms be able to bid for public works or for telecommunications contracts and expect to be treated in the same way as European-Community firms?

The answer appears to be no. Services are not covered by GATT, public procurement only imperfectly so. The Community's hands are not tied. So in this area Mr. de Clercq is relatively unambiguous: "Where international obligations do not exist, as for example in the field of services, we see no reason why the benefits of our internal liberalization should be extended unilaterally to third countries. We shall be ready and willing to negotiate reciprocal concessions with third countries, preferably in a multilateral context but also bilaterally. We want to open our borders, but on the basis of a mutual balance of advantages in the spirit of the GATT."[10]

On the surface, there is nothing to object to in this formulation. In fact, the Community may well use its bargaining power positively to prise open other markets in the service sector, rather like the United States may do in Section 301 investigations. If so, so much the better. The Single Market may have a "tin-opener" effect, as the Community trades on other countries' desire to improve their access to its many millions of high-income consumers.

However, the reference to bilateral agreements is not entirely reassuring. And a very large question mark hovers over what exactly is meant by reciprocity. There are currently three possible interpretations.

Conventional Reciprocity. In the GATT context, for instance, this would refer to the tariff-bargaining process whereby negotiators would agree to cut tariffs across the board by similar amounts according to some formula, which in their estimation would impose a roughly equal "effort" on each partner. The purpose, in the old days, was to improve market access, and major players like the United States and the European Community would announce at the end of the negotiation that they had offered tariffs cuts on $X million worth of imports and had obtained tariff concessions on $X+Y million worth of exports. This made the negotiation sound successful, but nobody would take the figures very seriously (except perhaps the negotiators) because there was no way of knowing how trade would flow in the future, or what the future incremental effect on imports and exports of a trade negotiation would be. Smaller countries would make similar calculations and those of them that adopted a "free rider" attitude in the multilateral GATT setting would be able to return home with an even better own-cuts/concession ratio. In the end, as an economic approach to the problem of reciprocity could have told them in the first place, both imports and exports grew in rough proportion to each other, any noticeable imbalance being due to macroeconomic variables rather than microeconomic tariff policy.

If the EC is prepared to negotiate in the service sector on the basis of conventional reciprocity, all will be well. The terms would be somewhat different from old-fashioned GATT-type tariff reciprocity. They would be somewhat along these lines: the subsidiaries of American, Austrian or Japanese banks are free to establish themselves in London or Paris, and will be treated just like Community banks, on condition that any Community bank that wishes to set up in the United States, Austria or Japan is free to do so and will be treated just like a U.S., Austrian or Japanese bank. This applies the principle of national treatment to foreign firms and is the equivalent of complete free trade in the international commerce of goods.

Volume Reciprocity. We have already referred to the disturbing trend in international trade talks today towards sectoral negotiations in a bilateral setting. Take EC-Japan discussions on automobiles, EC-U.S. negotiations on information technology or U.S.-Japanese talks on microprocessors, to name only a few ongoing "problems." From the little that transpires of these negotiations, one thing is clear: "reciprocity" is discussed in terms of a bilateral balancing of trade flows or, if balancing is out of the question (as in the case of the EC-Japan discussions over motorcars), then in terms of some "improvement" in the existing imbalance. For instance, the EC automobile manufacturers want the Community to insist that Japan should raise its share of imported European cars to 5 percent of the Japanese market, before allowing Japan to increase its current 10 percent share of the European market.

While this strikes a chord in the hearts of all European automobile manufacturers and a great many of their satisfied customers, who view this as only "fair," it send shudders down the spines of those with some knowledge of the implications of bilateralism in international trade. Bilateralism destroyed the trade system in the 1930s and could do so again in the future. It is incompatible with market-driven trade, involves direct state intervention in managing trade flows (implying quotas and/ or subsidies to achieve bilateral balance) and ends up in corporatist cartels, with government and big business managing trade flows to their convenience. (See the South Korean case cited above, footnote 15.) How else can one stop South Korean businessmen from selling to eager Europeans? How else can one force Japanese consumers to buy European cars? In the end, because this is in fact impossible in a free society, bilateralism ends up by cutting back trade until it fits the Procrustean bed of the least efficient trade partner's trade flows.

Applying the concept of "volume reciprocity" to the service sector would look something like this: the EC will be glad to extend hospitality to five Japanese banks to conduct operations of the type a, b and c (perhaps limited to the geographic area of France, the Netherlands and the U.K., which together make up a market roughly similar in size to Japan's) on condition Tokyo gives five European banks a similar charter to be active in Japan on a comparable basis, the whole agreement to be subject to annual review to make sure that the five banks on each side conduct roughly the same volume of business.

The end result of this approach would be that the subsidiaries of American, Japanese and other non-Community banks would not be treated "just like" Community banks, but they would not be completely excluded from the EC either. The extent of their rights would depend on how much Tokyo or Washington could offer in exchange (and Washington, as we know, can offer very little in terms of banking because of the Glass-Steagall Act . . .). Large countries would fare better than small ones, because they could offer "more." Switzerland, for instance, with its population of only 6 million people and a federal structure to boot, would find it very difficult to negotiate meaningful entry into the EC on the basis of "volume reciprocity."

Finally, we have something that might be called *extraterritorial reciprocity*. It is the notion that the EC would be prepared to treat the subsidiaries of U.S., Japanese or Swiss banks just like EC banks, provided the United States, Japan and Switzerland accorded the subsidiaries of EC banks in their markets the same privileges the EC offers *their* subsidiaries in *its* market. In other words, the EC would be exporting its notion of mutual recognition of banking regulations. If the United States continued to insist on hampering the development of branch banking across the United States or to prevent commercial and investment banking from taking place within the same firms, that would be its own problem, but the Glass-Steagall Act would not apply to European banks, because the United States would "recognize" as valid the European approach to banking regulation.

If this sounds fanciful, consider the following quotation, which is very carefully worded and which could apply to any one of these three notions of reciprocity:

> Our view is that Community credit institutions should have equal access to the financial markets of non-Community countries. Therefore, at the stage of the initial authorization of a non-Community institution in a member state, the Commission will check on a case-by-case basis whether similar institutions from all member states are given the same treatment in the non-Community country concerned. If not, the authorization pro-

cedure will be suspended until we have ensured reciprocity by negotiating with the non-Community country concerned. (What exactly is meant by "equal access," by "the same treatment"?)

In general terms, what we wish to do is to provide ourselves with negotiating leverage with which to pursue our general aim of overall reciprocity. . . .

Access to sensitive areas such as the right of establishment, services and a number of public procurement sectors, will depend on the realization of a satisfactory degree of reciprocity.

EFTA countries have always given me to understand that they have no problem with the concept of reciprocity . . . however, there are bound to be areas . . . where it will be *difficult to establish a balance between advantages and obligations.*[11] (Emphasis added—this last phrase being an unusually clear warning that the EC intends to use the notion of volume reciprocity.)

Time will tell which notion of reciprocity will predominate, but if the first is too liberal and the last too fanciful, then there are no prizes for guessing which one we will end up with. And "volume" reciprocity is just another name for bilateral balancing, the most protectionist and interventionist trade system ever invented.

The Future of Multilateralism

The multilateral GATT system is falling apart because it is no longer perceived as "fair" or reciprocal. Now economists tend to be rather patronizing about reciprocity (even about the "conventional reciprocity" just described: why insist on equivalent tariff cuts between trade partners, since tariff-cutting is good for you?) and they certainly view "fair" trade as being the first and last refuge of the protectionist. However, we live in a political world and a trading system has to be founded on some notion of reciprocity if it is to survive politically.

For various reasons, which are well known and will not detain us here, a great many members of GATT have not participated actively in 40 years of attempts to reduce barriers to trade. In fact, many were explicitly invited to make no contribution to liberalization, even after across-the-board methods of trade bargaining were developed and perfected. Instead, they were even given trade preferences on infant-industry-stimulation grounds.

As a result of many reasons, which again will not detain us here, industrial development has spread across the globe—by no means evenly, by no means always as a result of pure "market" processes—but it has spread. A great many developing countries now have a stake in the international trade system, but contribute little to it. Many of them have promoted industrial development behind high tariffs—with greater and lesser success, of course, but that is not the point. The point is that even the rather more outward-looking industrializing countries have high levels of protection and find it just as difficult to cope with local business interests as developed countries do. So why should they change their tariff structure, especially as the GATT system does not oblige them to do so?

U.S. concern with "level playing fields," which has been turned into concrete action by Section 301 negotiations, is the latest and most obvious consequence of this state of affairs. The EC's liberal use of antidumping investigations is another. If one kicks reciprocity out of one door, it comes back in again through another—but in a sinister bilateral disguise.

So how can one create a political constituency for a freer and *multilateral* trade system? I can only reiterate a proposal we have already made in 1986: to form an open-ended free trade area among the "traders" in the GATT.[12] A self-selected group of countries, which would include both developed and developing nations, and which are interested in promoting trade on a "fair" and reciprocal basis, should identify themselves and work toward a really spectacular objective, such as free trade among themselves by the end of the century.

Such a free trade agreement, subject to Article XXIV of GATT, could be flexible in terms of coverage and as well as membership, but in one respect it would be quit rigid: each member would have to commit itself to progressive, automatic liberalization of its import regime toward imports from partner countries. However, as all others would be doing the same, the political pain of one's own liberalization would be balanced by the political gain of one's partners' liberalization. Why else are customs unions and free trade areas such a popular vehicle of trade policy? Because they guarantee reciprocity on a grand scale. If the free trade area included all the developed world, plus some developing countries, it would be so large that trade diversion would not be a problem.

It is naturally understood that this is a second-best solution, and that unilateral free trade not based on reciprocity might be preferable. *However*, given that the first-best solution is not available, this second-best proposal not only offers the prospect of net trade creation based on specialization within the group, but also sets up what we have called the "dynamics of discrimination." In other words, for countries wavering between being "traders" or "nontraders," the fear of being discriminated against would probably overcome their hesitations, and they would join too. This would leave only the genuine "non-traders" out of the system, but this is presumably what they want anyway. In the end, this open-ended free trade area would resemble the GATT *as it was originally conceived*, but it would contain, in addition, the ultimate objective of free trade among participating countries, which the initial GATT most definitely did not include.

The alternative to this route is all too easy to chart: the spread of regional free or freer-trade arrangements based on some kind of geo-political rationale; the spread of bilateralism; and the automatic exclusion of all new trade flows which disturb established producers. In other words, no trade system at all.

Notes

1. Speech by Willy de Clercq, "The European Community in a Changing World," Fundacion Jorge Esteban Roulet, Buenos Aires, 2 August 1988.

2. Speech by Willy de Clercq, "1992: The Impact on the Outside World," Europäisches Forum, Alpach, 29 August 1988.

3. Comuniqué, Meeting of Chiefs of State and Heads of Government, Hannover, June 1988.

4. See *Financial Times*, October 11, 1988, p. 8.

5. See, for instance, "South Korea seeks to curb exports to EC," *Financial Times*, October 6, 1988, p. 3. This report is perfectly explicit: "The increase (in South Korean exports to the EC in 1986–88) has led the European Commission to initiate several dumping investigations and to impose a recent dumping duty on South Korean videotape recorders. As a result, the Ministry of Commerce and Industry in Seoul has asked industrial associations to *monitor closely the sales performance* of any member-companies whose export increase to the EC exceeded 30 percent a year, and to *restrain any whose export increase went beyond 50 percent.*" . . . "In certain electronic products, South Korean companies *had been advised to stop selling to Europe altogether for a period.*" . . . "Both Seoul and Brussels officials *stress the unilateral and voluntary nature of the restraint.*" Can one be clearer?

6. If one works with the legal definition of dumping (sale at a price below the price practiced on the home market) one should be aware that it makes no sense economically. Competitive firms may well practice "dumping" for sound commercial reasons. In other words, in their view, they are not losing money over the transaction in the long run: they may be discriminating just in order to enter a new market and acquire market share rapidly—a perfectly justifiable competitive stance, fully available to all players in the market and not one which should be discouraged with anti-dumping duties. If one takes the more sophisticated view that dumping occurs if goods are sold below their *cost*, then one should be aware that in practice, unit cost is a very slippery concept. For instance, if one is speaking of modern products, containing certain research and development costs, the amount allocated to each unit is entirely arbitrary. Finally, one can be pretty sure that private firms, while they may indeed occasionally sell below cost to get rid of goods or to snatch markets away from their competitors, cannot sell below cost all the time. Private dumping is a self-

correcting phenomenon and in principle should not neet regulating. On the other hand, trade with state-planned economies is almost *definitionally* fraught with problems of dumping, because a state agency does not have to answer to the market.

7. See the Commission's Annual Report on the Community's Antidumping and Antisubsidy Activities. See also Japan's complaint to GATT concerning the 130 national quotas, referred to above.

8. Article XIX of GATT provides for emergency import restrictions to save local producers from the threat of "material injury." It is rarely used because the restrictions have to be introduced multilaterally. VERs and OMAs, on the other hand, can be neatly targeted at the particular producer which is causing the problem.

9. Article 58.

10. Speech by Willy de Clercq, "1992: The Impact on the Outside World," loc. cit.

11. Speech by Willy de Clercq, "1992: The Impact on the Outside World," loc. cit.

12. Gerard Curzon and Victoria Curzon Price, "Defusing Conflict between Traders and Non-traders," *The World Economy*, Vol. 9, No. 1, March 1986, pp. 19–36.

3

U.S. Policies Toward the GATT: Past, Present, Prospective

Jeffrey J. Schott

At the mid-point of the Uruguay Round of multilateral trade negotiations, prospects for comprehensive trade liberalization seem uncertain.
Longstanding merchandise trade barriers remain intractable, and new
barriers are being erected to offset exchange rate misalignments and to
pursue neomercantilist trade strategies. Large trade imbalances and heavy
debt-servicing burdens fuel protectionist pressures in developed and
developing countries. Trade, finance, and debt problems evoke protectionist pressures in developed and developing countries alike and seem
immune to resolution through the procedures set out in the General
Agreement on Tariffs and Trade (GATT).

As important, the major trading nations seem distracted from the
task at hand in Geneva. The promotion of bilateral and regional free
trade arrangements has gained great notoriety in Europe, Japan, and the
United States. Europeans focus on their own internal market reforms
under the 1992 initiative; Japan—beset by a continual stream of disputes
with its key trading partners on products ranging from rice to super-
computers—focuses on ways to better manage its bilateral trading
relationships with the United States and with other countries in the
Pacific Basin; and the United States, the *demandeur* of the Uruguay
Round, threatens to take unilateral actions under its "Super 301" provisions to open foreign markets to U.S. exports, and to pursue bilateral
or plurilateral trade pacts with "like-minded countries," if its lofty
objectives for the GATT talks are not met.

The recent negotiation of the Canada–United States Free Trade Agreement has reinforced U.S. interest in bilateral negotiations to promote

trade liberalization and to resolve longstanding trade disputes. Such an approach has been embraced both as a building block for broader multilateral agreements and as a fallback against a possible breakdown in GATT negotiations. However, the willingness of U.S. policymakers to actively explore prospects for "life after GATT" raises important questions about the U.S. commitment to the multilateral trading system. Will it continue to pursue free trade agreements (FTAs) with other countries or will it devote its efforts to the negotiation of new multilateral agreements in GATT in the Uruguay Round? Can it do both?

In response to these questions, this chapter will review U.S. policies toward the GATT from its conception through the current Uruguay Round of trade negotiations. The next section discusses U.S. influence on the formation of the GATT system, and the origin of current GATT problems, particularly with regard to agriculture and safeguards. The third and fourth sections trace the evolution of U.S. policies through three decades of trade negotiations, focusing on the two central themes of reciprocity and bilateralism/multilateralism. The fifth section examines the current status of the Uruguay Round, and prospective U.S. policies in key negotiating groups. The concluding section summarizes the common strains in U.S. policy over the past 50 years, and the challenge the United States and others face in reinvigorating the GATT trading system.

Origins of the GATT System

The benefits of open markets and free trade principles have been widely accepted as U.S. public policy since 1934. In that year—in response to the global depression in general and collapse of world trade in particular—the Congress enacted the Reciprocal Trade Agreements Act. The Act recognized the importance of open markets for economic growth, and called for renewed international efforts to rebuild world trading links through the negotiation of bilateral trade agreements.[1] The Act empowered the President to negotiate reductions of up to 50 percent in U.S. tariffs in the context of these pacts. The goal was simple and direct: increase world welfare through world trade.

The architects of the postwar era took this prescription to heart in planning for global economic recovery. The Bretton Woods institutions all sought to sponsor and secure peace through economic development and increased trade. This objective represented a rebirth of the Wilsonian ideal of "peace through trade" of a generation earlier, and underscored the strong American influence in the development of postwar global economic institutions.

The United States put forward the first proposals for an International Trade Organization (ITO) in December 1945, and multilateral negotiations began in London the following October.[2] In essence, its goal was the multilateral extension of the U.S. trade agreements program. The bilateral trade pacts negotiated by the United States during the preceding decade provided much of the fodder for the ITO draftsmen.

By the time the Draft Charter for an ITO was completed in 1948, however, the agreement—influenced by current economic and political developments—had taken a shape significantly different from the lofty ideals set out by its American forbears. War-torn and developing countries insisted on extensive safeguards for balance of payments reasons, and resisted U.S. efforts to craft strong rules to protect foreign direct investment from expropriation or discriminatory treatment. The negotiation of trading rules was clearly more sensitive politically than previous talks that established the International Monetary Fund and the World Bank; this factor increasingly complicated the drafting of the ITO as negotiations dragged on through the immediate postwar recession. As a result, the ITO Charter was much more nuanced and its obligations much less biting and binding than had been originally envisaged. This opened up the Charter to criticism both from the "perfectionists" who thought its provisions flawed, and from the "protectionists" who increasingly clamored for safeguards for national trading interests (Diebold 1952, 14–24).

Thus, even as liberal trade principles were being enshrined in the ITO, economic and political events cast doubts on the internationalist vision of 1945, and colored the U.S. debate over ratification of the ITO. Peace prospects were clouded by Soviet advances in Eastern Europe and revolution in China, and subsequently dashed outright by the Korean War; the slow economic recovery in Europe made it harder to press the case for an open world economy. Indeed, the Marshall Plan focused immediate attention on aid, not trade, recognizing the long-term horizon of trade reform.[3]

In the United States, postwar recession and unemployment raised doubts as to the wisdom of leaving U.S. markets unprotected against foreign competition. GNP in real terms dropped precipitously in 1946 and then averaged only 0.3 percent annual growth for the next three years. Unemployment rose by more than 2 million between 1945 and 1949.

In addition, U.S. business groups lobbied hard against perceived weaknesses in the Charter itself. Interestingly, many of their concerns still resonate in the contemporary debate in the Uruguay Round. A key concern involved the pervasive loopholes from ITO obligations that were available for countries suffering balance of payments (BOP) problems.

Presciently, it was argued that such BOP safeguards would lead to quasi-permanent import controls.[4] Other problems related to omissions or weakness in ITO provisions regarding investment and restrictive business practices—concerns that echo in current U.S. demands for expanded coverage of GATT discipline.

However, the United States was itself partly to blame for weaknesses in the ITO structure. Agricultural provisions and the safeguards clause were dictated by the prevailing practices and political pressures in the United States. The weakness of obligations in these areas has come back to haunt the United States in recent years; it is a legacy that current negotiators in the Uruguay Round are seeking to undo. As such, each deserves a brief elaboration.

Agriculture. Since the Agricultural Adjustment Act of 1933, U.S. farm policy has involved a mixture of price supports, production controls and export subsidies, and deficiency payments (i.e., income supports). The United States insisted that the ITO and the GATT contain special rules for agriculture to protect its domestic farm programs. The trading rules were designed to fit the existing practices (Hathaway 1987, chap. 5). Even so, the United States had to obtain a waiver of GATT rules in 1955 to provide cover for import quotas needed to underpin programs for sugar, peanuts, and dairy products under section 22 of the Agricultural Adjustment Act of 1933. This "temporary" waiver still is in effect today, and has posed a significant obstacle to efforts to reform GATT rules on agricultural subsidies. With the advent of the common agricultural policy in Europe, another vested interest arose to block the extension of GATT reforms to agriculture.

As a result, GATT rules allow countries (1) to impose trade and production controls to support arbitrary domestic farm prices above world market levels, and (2) to use export subsidies to compete in world markets. Exceptions to the general prohibition on quantitative restrictions were added to GATT Article XI so that countries could impose import controls to defend farm price support programs, and agricultural subsidies were subject to almost no discipline under GATT Article XVI. Even when Article XVI was amended in 1955, the provisions regarding subsidies on primary products (including agriculture) sought only to avoid the use of subsidies if they would result in that country gaining "more than an equitable share of world trade" (Article XVI:3). Attempts were later made to clarify that provision in the Tokyo Round Subsidies Code, but the results were mostly cosmetic.

The vagueness of GATT rules on agriculture has sparked numerous trade disputes, especially in the past decade. Overproduction of key crops has led to widespread dumping in world markets, and subsidy wars have erupted, as countries have fought to maintain or win market share. Producers and taxpayers have been the victims of the price depressing consequences of such policies. GATT panels generally have been unable to adjudicate the resulting disputes because of the imprecision of GATT obligations. More important, the lack of political will to reform farm programs significantly has both exacerbated the disputes and impugned the credibility of GATT procedures in general.

Safeguards. The inclusion of an escape clause in trade agreements has been a prerequisite for agreement on trade liberalization since the 1930s trade agreements program. The U.S.-Mexico agreement in 1943 provided a model for the negotiation of GATT Article XIX, which is designed to provide temporary relief from import competition that causes or threatens serious injury to domestic producers (Destler 1986, 20). However, the terms and conditions for invoking Article XIX are vague, and the recourse available to the exporting and other affected third countries—either compensation or retaliation—has led countries to avoid the invocation of Article XIX safeguards altogether.

In short, the escape clause was meant to promote trade reforms; the weaknesses in its elaboration have led instead to its disuse and substitution by a rash of extra-GATT import controls and by the zealous use of antidumping duties. The result is often the imposition of voluntary export restraints (VERs), applied to key sectors such as textiles and apparel, steel, and autos.[5] In many respects, VERs have become the most pernicious form of trade control.

* * *

In this atmosphere, it is not surprising that ratification of the ITO was never acted on by the U.S. Congress. In December 1950, the ITO was quietly withdrawn from consideration by President Truman and never resubmitted. Instead, the United States settled for a slimmed-down version of the ITO Charter, the General Agreement on Tariffs and Trade, that had served as an interim trade agreement and forum for three rounds of multilateral tariff negotiations from 1947 to 1951.

As John Jackson has noted, "GATT was drafted with the express assumption that an ITO would materialize" (Jackson 1969, 50). As such, it lacked institutional structure and a comprehensive set of rules and obligations needed to discipline international trade. The structural flaws have become increasingly serious as the growth of world trade and the growing interdependence of national economies have put mounting demands on the GATT system.

The GATT has never been consented to by the Senate as a treaty obligation of the United States. Technically, it is an executive agreement concluded under the authority provided the President in the Reciprocal Trade Agreement Act of 1934, as amended (Jackson 1969, chap. 2).

While recognizing U.S. GATT obligations, the Congress has used this fact to distance itself politically from the GATT; indeed, "Congress made it plain that it was not endorsing GATT when it extended the Trade Agreements Act in 1951" (Diebold 1952, 28). This was a clear indication that the U.S. political commitment to liberal trade principles had its bounds.

Reciprocity and the GATT

"Reciprocity" has been a central theme of U.S. trade policy since the passage of the Reciprocal Trade Agreements Act of 1934, and has been a pillar of U.S. participation in the GATT system. In an important sense, reciprocity is a relative term defined by negotiation, that is, whatever bargain is struck is by its nature reciprocal. In the early rounds of GATT tariff negotiations, the United States was quite generous in the terms that it accepted from its trading partners. However, as the relative predominance of U.S. trade diminished with the growth of Europe and Japan, the U.S. reciprocity standard became increasingly more demanding. Moreover, as negotiations began to involve more than tariff cuts, the calculation of reciprocity became more complicated and more subjective.

The end of the Kennedy Round was a turning point for the GATT. The successful tariff negotiation lowered average duties to single digits in all the major trading countries, but at the same time exposed insidious layers of protectionism imbedded in domestic programs and regulations. Such nontariff barriers (NTBs) frustrated market access and undercut the value of the tariff concessions negotiated in the Kennedy Round. GATT provisions were inadequate to deal with these problems. The only attempt to develop new trading rules to discipline NTBs, the Antidumping Code negotiated during the Kennedy Round, was undercut soon after the Round when the Congress rejected conforming changes in domestic procedures of U.S. trade laws.

The new focus on NTBs coincided with the period of dollar depreciation, the collapse of the Bretton Woods system of fixed exchange rates, and the growing competitiveness of European and Japanese firms. The U.S. trade balance fell into deficit in 1971 for the first time since 1894. Protectionist pressures coalesced in the U.S. Congress around the Burke-Hartke bill, characterized by its opponents as the second coming of the infamous Smoot-Hawley bill of 1930.

The Burke-Hartke bill was essentially a protectionist reaction to the Kennedy Round results. With strong support from U.S. labor unions, it sought to erect quotas on U.S. imports, and to accord additional powers to domestic agencies to determine whether imports were benefiting from unfair trade practices.

While Burke-Hartke did not become law, it did influence the development of subsequent U.S. trade legislation, in particular the Trade Act of 1974. The reciprocity standard was recast; a "level playing field" for U.S. trading interests became the goal of U.S. trade policy. Instead of relative reciprocity, U.S. negotiators began to push for "substantially equivalent competitive opportunities."

The Congress fought long and hard before deciding how to implement that goal. The unilateral approach of Burke-Hartke was rejected in favor of new multilateral trade negotiations. But it took almost two years of debate to craft implementing legislation for such talks before the Trade Act of 1974 was signed on 3 January 1975, more than 15 months after the Tokyo ministerial declaration of September 1973 had launched the new GATT round. The result was a substantial elaboration of U.S. trade law that both reconfirmed and complicated U.S. participation in the Tokyo Round.

The Trade Act of 1974 provided all the authorities the Ford administration needed to enter into the Tokyo Round negotiations. The President was given proclamation authority to cut most tariffs by 50 percent, and was encouraged to negotiate new codes of conduct on NTBs. The Act also gave a mandate for U.S. efforts to craft new rules on trade in services. In addition, to ensure that the Act's provisions on countervailing duties (CVDs) would not disrupt ongoing GATT negotiations seeking new disciplines on subsidies, the President also was accorded the authority to waive the imposition of CVDs in certain circumstances.

Perhaps most importantly, given the experience of the Antidumping Code after the Kennedy Round, the Act introduced new procedures for expeditious implementation of NTB agreements. Under the so-called "fast track," the President was empowered to submit legislation to implement NTB agreements that would be subject to expedited consideration, no amendments, and approval by a simple majority (see Destler 1986, 62–69). The fast-track provisions were conditioned by an intricate set of notification and consultation requirements with the Congress to ensure that Congressional concerns were reflected in the negotiation of the NTB pacts. Today, such procedures are deemed so essential to Congressional passage of trade agreements that they are commonly regarded as part of the President's implicit negotiating authority.

At the same time, however, the Congress insisted that the United States defend its trading interests while GATT talks proceeded. Emphasis was placed on unilateral actions that could be taken without resort to the lengthy and often ambiguous GATT consultative and dispute settlement mechanisms. The Trade Act adopted new domestic procedures that promoted greater automaticity in the application of U.S. unfair trade statutes and introduced new authority to enforce U.S. rights under international trade agreements. Under section 301 of the Trade Act of 1974, almost any foreign practice could be subject to U.S. retaliation if it were construed as "unreasonable, unjustifiable, or discriminatory"— a very open-ended standard. In practice, however, presidents have been quite cautious in applying this statute for fear of disrupting world trade and impairing U.S. obligations under the GATT.

Thus, while promoting the new Tokyo Round, the United States hedged its bets by elaborating new import control policies. Such an approach could be regarded as pragmatic—that is, negotiating from a position of strength. However, it also represented a growing U.S. concern that GATT did not provide effective discipline on foreign trade practices and that strong unilateral action may be required to enforce U.S. rights under international trade agreements.

There is nothing wrong with aggressively protecting the rights of U.S. trading interests under international trade agreements. Without such enforcement, the efficacy of trade concessions is questioned, and the ability to negotiate new agreements is compromised.

In some cases, the increased use of 301 actions can have beneficial effects. Bilateral pressure can coerce countries into liberalizing their import barriers, allowing them to overcome domestic political opposition to actions that could hurt the protected sector but increase the welfare to the economy as a whole. In this respect, 301 actions—used as a threat—can support the objectives of the multilateral system.

However, the use of 301 procedures can also have perverse results. First, the United States has sometimes sought preferential access for its suppliers in foreign markets. This can result merely in the substitution of U.S. goods for imports from other countries (as occurred when Japan increased the U.S. beef import quota and effectively cut Australian imports through changes in its buy-sell system), and it can lead to rigid market-sharing arrangements that decrease pressure for trade liberalization. Once firms gain access to a protected market, the profits they earn lead them to oppose further liberalization and competition (Bergsten et al. 1987).

Second, retaliation breeds retaliation. The main concern about retaliation is that, by its nature, it is trade restricting and can set in motion a tit-for-tat response that could unravel existing trading reforms.[6]

A third, and more serious, problem is emulation. Other countries often adopt U.S. trade practices as their own. The experience of the United States Export/Import Bank taught the Japanese and others the not-so-subtle art of subsidizing exports; similarly, U.S. antidumping and countervail practices have been adopted in several countries. Most recently, the European Community adopted in 1984 a "new commercial instrument" modeled after U.S. section 301. Not surprisingly, the first cases under that provision were directed against alleged unfair practices by the United States.

Finally, the section 301 approach allows the United States to judge unilaterally whether trade agreements are being followed. In 301, as in exports controls, the U.S. list of "actionable" practices is far larger than that of its trading partners.[7] If the 301 threat is exercised, as in the semiconductor case against Japan, the unilateral action may violate GATT rules (which require *multilateral* authorization), lead to the cartelization of markets, and increase trade barriers.[8]

The results of Tokyo Round initially were hailed as a triumph for the GATT and for the forces of "fair trade." Six NTB codes were negotiated, covering domestic practices such as subsidies and CVDs, antidumping, public procurement, and technical standards, as well as customs valuation and import licensing. In judging the results, the U.S. Congress focused most prominently on the GATT Subsidies Code. Implementing provisions for that agreement alone accounted for a substantial part of the Trade Agreements Act of 1979, which—under the fast-track procedures of the 1974 Trade Act—passed the Congress by overwhelming majorities and was signed into law on 26 July 1979.

The U.S. Special Trade Representative, Robert S. Strauss, perhaps did too good a job in selling the Tokyo Round results to Congress. Soon after, the combination of the second oil shock, soaring interest rates, the subsequent global recession, and a severe debt crisis in several key developing countries had a sharp contractionary effect on world trade. In 1981 and 1982 world trade declined in value and volume terms, and countries refocused trade policy toward protection of industries and the maintenance of jobs. Implementation of Tokyo Round trade reforms was side-tracked, as countries tried to "export" unemployment—i.e., supporting domestic production through increased (and often subsidized or dumped) foreign sales. LDC subsidy commitments unraveled as those countries promoted exports to earn hard currencies to service their debts.

For the first time, GATT members were confronted with the dilemma of how to implement trade liberalization in a period of economic stagnation. The U.S. solution was to push for the start of a new round of GATT negotiations, which—true to the "bicycle theory" of trade liberalization—would deflect protectionist pressures and maintain momentum for trade reform. An extraordinary meeting of trade ministers convened for the first time in almost a decade in Geneva in November 1982.

In many respects, the 1982 Ministerial meeting was a near disaster for the GATT. The United States came to Geneva with a highly ambitious agenda for reforming agriculture and extending GATT discipline to services, investment, and new technologies. These goals were neither shared by other countries, nor were they adequately vetted prior to the Geneva meeting. The lack of consultations in preparation of the meeting only compounded the confusion and contributed to the unrealistic expectations of the U.S. delegation. The anodyne declaration that emerged from five days of negotiations did little to restore confidence in GATT processes. Ambassador Brock left Geneva with a bad taste for GATT negotiations, and began to encourage complementary bilateral talks. Congressional representatives at the ministerial came away with even greater skepticism about the efficacy of GATT rules and procedures, and more convinced of the need to pursue unilateral measures to defend U.S. trading interests.[9]

Bilateralism Versus Multilateralism

The GATT has always had an inherent tension between bilateral and multilateral negotiations. Besides being a body of multilateral trading rules and a forum for multilateral negotiations, the GATT is a repository of each member's schedule of trade concessions. These concessions are negotiated bilaterally but generally applied to all signatories under the GATT's most-favored-nation principle. Bilateral negotiations thus are an integral part of the GATT negotiating process.

While the United States continues to be a strong supporter of the multilateral trading system, it has not put all its eggs in the GATT basket. In recent years, the United States has become impatient with the pace of GATT talks, and dissatisfied with the effectiveness of GATT rules and dispute settlement procedures in protecting U.S. trading interests. This concern is particularly strong in the Congress, where the residue of ill-will generated by the failure of the 1982 GATT Ministerial meeting still colors attitudes toward the GATT.

In addition, and perhaps more importantly, U.S. trade policy has been driven in the 1980s by the need to manage the protectionist pressures generated by job losses (particularly in the manufacturing sector) and mounting U.S. trade deficits. To counter these pressures and sustain domestic support for an open trade policy, the United States has resorted to a mixture of bilateral and plurilateral approaches to help build a multilateral consensus for trade reforms, and to resolve trade disputes and to remove trade barriers (Baker 1988).[10]

In essence, bilateralism has been used to close up the leaks in the multilateral system until permanent solutions could be negotiated in the GATT. As noted above, this approach is not necessarily inconsistent with the spirit or letter of the GATT; indeed, the objective has been to sustain political support for an open trade policy and GATT negotiations. The policy has been implemented through a combination of unilateral actions and bilateral negotiations (see Diebold 1988).

First, the United States has attempted to use its economic clout (i.e., the threat of closing U.S. markets to countries that do not provide reciprocal market access for U.S. exporters) to liberalize foreign trade barriers. Negotiations have taken place with Japan on beef, citrus, and semiconductors and with Korea on insurance and cigarettes, among others. This approach relies heavily on threatened resort to the retaliatory provisions of section 301 of the Trade Act of 1974 (and on bilateral accords) than on GATT procedures. It was adopted by the Reagan administration (prompted by Congressional pressure) in large measure because it satisfies the political demand for action on trade policy and for more expedited negotiations than seem possible in the multilateral forum of the GATT. This approach has now been codified in the new Omnibus Trade and Competitiveness Act, signed into law on 23 August 1988.

Second, the United States has negotiated bilateral free trade agreements (FTAs) with Israel and Canada to promote trade liberalization among "like-minded" countries and to lay a foundation for broader multilateral arrangements. As such, this approach has attempted to build a consensus for GATT reforms, especially in new areas such as services and investment.

The U.S.-Canada FTA is illustrative of a bilateral agreement that promotes both U.S. economic interests and the multilateral trading system. The FTA provides a counterweight to the protectionist trend worldwide and thus gives a big boost to GATT efforts to liberalize trade. Furthermore, the FTA contains provisions, especially in areas such as services, investment, and dispute settlement, that could serve as models for prospective GATT accords under negotiation in the Uruguay Round (Schott 1988). Because of its stimulus to growth in the North American market, and the absence of new barriers to third-country trade, the trade-creating effects of the FTA should far outdistance the trade-diverting consequences of the FTA preferences. As such the FTA should conform fully to the requirements of GATT Article XXIV (which sanctions such preferential pacts in specific circumstances).

Could the U.S.-Canada FTA be replicated with other countries? Several countries have already expressed an interest in exploring such an arrangement with the United States. Studies are underway in Japan, Korea, and the ASEAN in response to initial U.S. overtures for a possible FTA. Australia previously studied and rejected a bilateral FTA with the United States (Snape 1986). In addition, Mexico has proposed a less comprehensive bilateral agreement with the United States involving liberalization in particular industrial and service sectors. However, no one has taken a close look at what would be involved in such prospective

FTAs, including the U.S. barriers that might have to be removed and the implications for the world trading system.[11]

Interestingly, the most attention has been given to a possible U.S.-Japan FTA, the agreement *least likely* to be negotiated.[12] Such a pact would pose major political problems in both countries. In particular, Japan would have a hard time including agricultural liberalization—a key U.S. objective. In addition, many other domestic policies that affect trade and are high on the U.S. agenda for bilateral talks—such as antitrust policies—would fall beyond the pale of trade negotiations.

Privately, Japanese officials have cautioned against a full-blown trade agreement. Instead, they would like to use the Mansfield invitation to explore ways to improve the management of the U.S.-Japan trade relationship. In that regard, the dispute settlement provisions of the U.S.-Canada FTA seem to be of particular interest to the Japanese (and to others as well).

As a practical matter, however, it would be very difficult in any event to negotiate a FTA as comprehensive as the U.S.-Canada agreement. In many respects, the U.S.-Canada FTA is unique:

- there already is substantial integration of the two economies, including cross-ownership in key sectors such as autos and affiliated unions in steel and textiles and apparel;
- the FTA does not impose significant adjustment pressures on politically-powerful industries such as textiles, apparel and steel (in part because there is not a great disparity in wage rates); and
- there already is substantial convergence of key trade-related regulatory policies (e.g., countervailing duty laws; trend towards deregulation of financial markets).

No other "candidate" FTA would have these advantages or could realistically meet the GATT tests. U.S. labor unions would complain about wage disparities, and import-sensitive industries such as steel and textiles would balk at the liberalization of their quotas that undoubtedly would be required to secure an agreement.

As a result, prospective agreements would likely evolve into *sectoral* FTAs in which the balance between trade creation and trade diversion would be less distinct. Such *sectoral* FTAs would not be consistent with the three-part test for FTAs set out in GATT Article XXIV: that the FTA covers substantially all trade between the partner countries, that it is trade-creating, and that it does not raise new barriers to third country trade. As such, they would require waivers under GATT Article XXV (as the United States obtained for the 1965 U.S.-Canada Auto Pact).

However, the proliferation of such waivers could do extensive damage to the multilateral fabric of the GATT system. The reason is straightforward: bilateral agreements discriminate against nonparticipants while the GATT system is based on the principle of nondiscrimination. GATT provisions only allow exceptions to this principle if FTAs and customs unions meet the three-part test noted above.

Moreover, the benefits of such agreements for the United States could well be transitory. Where past U.S. efforts to open foreign markets have succeeded, they have often resulted in special preferences for U.S. suppliers to the detriment of other exporters. Indeed, at times U.S. pressure has only resulted in a redistribution of import shares and not overall liberalization. However, such efforts inevitably are imitated by other countries seeking their own special deals. In the end, such actions often result in market-sharing arrangements instead of market liberalization—an outcome that is clearly inferior to the maintenance of GATT for U.S. trading interests.

The Canada–United States FTA seems to be the exception that proves the rule that bilateral FTAs between the United States and other countries are not consistent with a strong multilateral trading system. In the near term, U.S. negotiating efforts will continue to be directed primarily at liberalizing trade and strengthening the GATT system in the context of the Uruguay Round. Exploratory talks may be held on prospective FTAs, but they will be regarded as a fallback—and distinctly suboptimal to the GATT system—in the event the Uruguay Round falters.

A possible exception to this approach could be the negotiation of a bilateral trade agreement with Mexico. The political, economic and social benefits of such an accord arguably could justify the extension of discriminatory preferences to Mexico. Given the fact that Mexico already conducts the predominant share of its trade with the United States, a prospective FTA with Mexico—whether sectoral or comprehensive— would probably not result in significant trade diversion and thus would not likely undercut the broader effort to secure multilateral trade liberalization.

The Uruguay Round

In September 1986, trade ministers met in Punta del Este, Uruguay, and issued a declaration that formally launched the "Uruguay Round" of GATT negotiations. Recognizing the protectionist threat to the GATT and the need "to develop a more open, viable and durable multilateral trading system," the ministers agreed on a broadbased agenda encompassing both the traditional areas of GATT competence and new issues such as services, investment, and intellectual property rights.

The United States led the fight to launch the Uruguay Round; at Punta, it was joined by coalitions of countries—developed and developing alike—that recognized that the success of the new round was crucial to counter the trend toward bilateralism and to reform and reinvigorate the multilateral trading system. Indeed, it was the recognition by the second and third level powers in GATT that, if the erosion of GATT discipline was not halted and reversed, they would be the most severe victims of growing protectionism in the United States, Europe, and Japan, that overcame opposition to the new round by a small group of ideologically-bent developing countries.

Success will be difficult to achieve by the scheduled completion date of December 1990. The Uruguay Round agenda is full of problems that have resisted reform over the past seven rounds of negotiations (e.g., agricultural subsidies; voluntary export restraints and other quotas) as well as new issues (e.g., services, trade-related investment measures and intellectual property rights) where the United States and others seek to extend the scope and coverage of GATT discipline to an important share of world trade.

The difficulty of the task became evident in the mid-term review of the negotiations in Montreal in December 1988. While interim agreements were reached in 11 of the 15 GATT negotiating groups, the talks stalled over agriculture, safeguards, textiles and apparel, and intellectual property rights (IPRs). The Uruguay Round went into remission until April 1989, when agreements in these four areas cleared away the remaining *procedural* roadblocks to the substantive or "hard-bargaining" phase of the negotiations.

Through April 1989, U.S. efforts in the Uruguay Round have centered on agriculture, services, IPRs, and institutional issues—including dispute settlement procedures—designed to strengthen the GATT framework. By contrast, U.S. negotiators have been almost devout in their silence on textiles and apparel, and relatively circumspect in their proposals on subsidies, safeguards, and trade-related investment issues.

Agriculture. Questions have been raised about why the United States gives agriculture—a sector that accounts for only 13 percent of world trade—such priority in the Uruguay Round. Part of the answer lies in domestic politics, as noted above. The farm sector had been the backbone of the open trade lobby in the United States, but support has weakened because of the combined impact of the overvalued dollar of the mid-1980s and ineffective GATT discipline on subsidies. Part of the answer may also lie in the not inconsequential fact that former U.S. Trade Representative and current Secretary of Agriculture Clayton Yeutter is a farmer from Nebraska. However, Dale Hathaway has emphasized three much more critical reasons:

- multilateral negotiations provide the most effective vehicle to stim-
  ulate needed reforms in national farm policies;
- current agricultural trade disputes damage the credibility of the
  GATT and undercut efforts to strengthen GATT discipline over all
  trade; and
- agricultural trade disputes threaten trade in other products since
  retaliation does not necessarily have to be limited to "like products"
  (Hathaway 1987, 2).

For these reasons, substantive results in the agricultural negotiations are
crucial to the overall success of the Uruguay Round. Unlike the Kennedy
and Tokyo Rounds, the United States is unlikely to agree to a Uruguay
Round package without a strong component of agricultural trade reforms.

Bridging the wide gap between the United States and European
Community (EC) in this area, the Cairns group—a broadbased coalition
of agricultural exporting countries—has offered a sensible compromise,
consisting of both short-term and long-term policy reforms. The compromise reached in April 1989 essentially adopted the Cairns approach
in a two-step process: the negotiation of a standstill on subsidy programs
in the short-run, and then a subsequent schedule to scale back both
production and export subsidies over a fixed period of time. The latter
will require agreement on what types of trade-distorting practices should
be covered by the liberalization commitment and how the level of
subsidies should be calculated, i.e., based on producer subsidy equivalents
or other commodity-specific standards. Interestingly, the Cairns approach
is consistent with the limited policy reforms instituted in both the United
States and the EC in recent years.

Such commitments would require substantial changes over time in
existing farm programs, and would raise significant political challenges.
In the United States, the Bush administration will have to spell out to
Congress specifically what it wants, and what it is willing to pay for
foreign concessions. For example, the Congress will be loath to consider
reform of section 22 quotas until the President outlines to them what
he expects to get in return. Progress on agricultural issues will have to
be made early in the new administration before the Congress gets too
far along in drafting provisions of the prospective 1990 Farm Bill, thereby
constraining U.S. negotiating leverage in the GATT talks (Hathaway
1987 and *Reforming World Agricultural Trade* 1988).

Services. The United States has worked for more than a decade to
develop multilateral rules to discipline trade in services. Initial efforts
in the OECD Trade Committee in the mid-to-late 1970s were comple-
mented by extensive consultation on services in the GATT. Because of
the strong opposition in GATT, particularly from some key developing

countries, the United States had to exercise substantial leverage (including forcing a vote to ensure ministerial consideration of the issue) to get services on the GATT negotiating agenda, an effort that gave the mistaken impression that services was the number 1 U.S. negotiating priority in the Uruguay Round (see Schott and Mazza 1986).

While it is unlikely that the United States would accept a negotiated package that excluded new rules on services, U.S. negotiators recognize that—during the anticipated time frame of the Uruguay Round—it may not be possible to develop comprehensive disciplines covering a broad range of services sectors.[13] The United States has narrowed its sight on what can be achieved during the Uruguay Round from the expansive goals set out by U.S. Trade Representative William Brock in 1982 (see Brock 1982). Services remain a priority, but not *the* priority issue for the United States in the Uruguay Round.

What the United States is likely to work for in services is a two-part approach that establishes a framework agreement or "umbrella" code of principles to guide government policies followed by sectoral annotations delimiting the coverage of the agreements. However, the principles contained in the services code may not be universally applied because countries may not want to subject certain service sectors to code obligations. Therefore, flexibility may be needed in the range of concessions that countries are able to offer.

The provisions on services in the U.S.-Canada FTA provide a model of the type of framework agreement on services that the United States advocates for the GATT as well. FTA provisions establish firm contractual obligations regarding national treatment, establishment, and licensing and certification procedures. However, the U.S.-Canada agreement does little to liberalize existing restrictions on services trade. A successful GATT negotiation will require more tangible results in the form of liberalization of specific trade barriers.

Intellectual Property Rights. The United States first raised patent, trademark, and copyright issues in the waning days of the Tokyo Round. At that time, the focus was on a new code on commercial counterfeiting. While conclusion of such a pact is still strongly advocated, U.S. policy-makers have used this subject to press their agenda for high technology industries. As such, U.S. interests lie in the development of multilateral guidelines regarding protection *inter alia* for computer software, design masks for semiconductor chips, and biotechnologies, modeled after U.S. law, procedures, and legal precedents. The object is not to replace the World Intellectual Property Organization (WIPO), but rather to provide enforcement for established obligations and to develop new rules in areas where national IPR laws and regulations can have a trade-distorting impact.

The protection of IPRs is an area where the United States has made prominent use of section 301 procedures to exert bilateral pressure to reform national practices of its trading partners, partly due to its impatience with the pace of GATT deliberations and partly due to intolerance with the politically-charged procedures for reforming WIPO standards. Given the relative success of bilateral coercion, the United States is likely to continue to use 301 cases to help forge an international standard for IPR protection. Indeed, the only way to prevent U.S. bilateral efforts from proliferating may be to enact a GATT code that establishes effective and enforceable international disciplines.

Institutional Issues. It is not surprising that much of the focus of GATT talks in the Uruguay Round has been on issues such as surveillance of national trade policies, ministerial participation, and dispute settlement procedures. Reforms in these areas involve the *form* of the trade institution, not the *substance* of reciprocal trade negotiations, and do not directly affect domestic constituencies. Nonetheless, progress in these areas is essential if the United States and other GATT countries are to commit to meaningful trade reforms at the end of the Uruguay Round.

Significant progress has been achieved to date in the negotiating group on "Functioning of the GATT System" (FOGS) regarding trade policy reviews and greater ministerial participation in GATT affairs. Both these reforms were strongly advocated in the report of the GATT Wisemen in 1985 (Leutwiler et al. 1985). The third item on the FOGS agenda—involving trade/finance linkages—has not advanced very far, however. This last item holds great potential for reinforcing the institutional foundation of the GATT, and probably will receive more attention by U.S. negotiators in 1989–1990.

Reform of dispute settlement procedures has been a longstanding U.S. objective.[14] The United States worked hard in the Tokyo Round to elaborate new rules and procedures both in the Subsidies Code and as part of the Framework Agreement. In the Uruguay Round, it will try to build on these achievements, along with the innovative approaches set out in the U.S.-Canada FTA, to further improve the GATT dispute settlement mechanism.

The U.S. goal is to introduce more equity and objectivity to the dispute settlement process. Monitoring trade policies—as set out in the FOGS group—would help ensure greater conformity with GATT obligations and preempt some prospective problems. The information would also facilitate the preparation of more authoritative panel reports. Resort to binding arbitration—as set out in the U.S. Canada FTA—also would be a useful precedent for GATT reforms. With binding arbitration, countries would no longer be able to block the adoption of panel reports with impunity (see Horlick et al. 1988).

In addition, the introduction of surveillance of national trade policies—when combined with a more structured consultation and dispute settlement mechanism—could prove instructive for negotiators seeking to reinforce the GATT safeguards system. The new Trade Policy Review Mechanism could prove indispensable for monitoring compliance with prospective new safeguards obligations, especially if a new safeguards code requires adjustment by the industry benefiting from temporary protection (Hufbauer and Schott 1985).

The United States has given high priority to these institutional issues for two key reasons. First, confidence in the GATT's dispute settlement mechanism has to be restored; countries will be loath to commit to new trade liberalization if they believe their hard-won concessions will not be adequately enforced. Second, the lack of a strong institutional foundation casts doubt on the value of negotiating new trading rules—one does not graft new limbs on a sick tree.[15] Thus, U.S. efforts on services and other areas are predicated on enhanced institutional arrangements in the GATT.

Other Issues. In contrast to the Tokyo Round, U.S. efforts on *subsidies* have taken a much lower profile in the Uruguay Round. The United States seems to have lost faith in the Subsidies Code, and has sought to reopen the agreement to negotiate disciplines that were non-negotiable a decade earlier. This position reflects the dissatisfaction in Congress about the value of subsidy concessions gained in the Tokyo Round; many members feel they bought a "pig in a poke" in 1979 and now prefer to use the unilateral discipline of CVDs rather than GATT rules to attack foreign subsidies.[16]

In short, U.S. negotiators will be severely constrained in the subsidies area. Congress will be wary to accept any changes in U.S. subsidy/CVD practices unless significant reforms are accepted by the other major trading nations. The primary U.S. focus will be on the reduction of agricultural subsidies, both in the Code review and in the general negotiations on agriculture.

By contrast, the U.S. policy regarding *safeguards* is less constrained, but unfortunately has been no more imaginative than the approach taken in the 1970s that failed to produce agreement on a GATT Safeguards Code. Negotiators still are hung up on the "selectivity" issue, i.e., whether safeguards actions should be applied against all countries or only a select few, as well as the related problem of Code coverage of "gray area measures" such as voluntary export restraints (VERs). These issues are related because most safeguard actions now take the form of VERs. While such measures *appear* to be selective, in fact VERs often have to be extended to almost all suppliers to prevent leakage through uncovered countries. As such, VERs have become a vehicle to globalize trade restraints in textiles and apparel, steel, and perhaps soon in autos (in Europe). Resolution of both problems is needed to induce countries to impose trade restrictions pursuant to GATT Article XIX instead of outside the GATT system.

To achieve discipline on VERs will require commensurate discipline on the safeguard practices of other countries, however. As such, it is possible that the United States will seek to link reform of Article XIX with new discipline on the BOP safeguards afforded under Article XVIII. For such an approach to be meaningful, however, the major industrial countries would have to begin to unravel longstanding trade barriers to Third World exports, and, in particular, to reform or phase out the Multi-Fiber Arrangement (MFA).

On this last issue, U.S. negotiators have maintained an awkward silence—but for a very good reason. Congressional actions on *textiles and apparel* have sought to globalize, not liberalize, trade controls. Indeed, the recent U.S. textiles bill sought to limit the annual growth of imports from major suppliers to one percent. The legislation passed Congress handily, although the size of the margin was in large part because Congress knew that the President would veto the bill—and could sustain that veto—in the closing days of the Congress.

The Bush administration will face countervailing pressures at home and abroad to reform the regime of import protection for textiles and apparel. Seeking a gradual phase-out of the MFA would be strongly resisted by U.S. industry, but would increase dramatically the ante for trade liberalization and thereby enhance prospects for the U.S. objectives on safeguards noted above.[17] The willingness of developing countries to liberalize their trade barriers will hinge importantly on the ability of the United States, Europe, and Japan to begin to unravel trade protection for textiles and apparel, and other products. The challenge will be to devise strategies that accommodate the adjustment needs of domestic industry while committing to a gradual phase-out of longstanding trade barriers and a return to GATT rules for textiles and apparel.

Finally, U.S. negotiators will continue to push for new rules to cover trade-related *investment* measures (TRIMs). To date, the talks have focused on investment incentives and performance requirements—measures that can have significant trade effects. The issue of establishment rights has provoked more controversy. Overall, however, the TRIMs negotiations have not generated extensive interest among GATT delegations.

The U.S. approach to the TRIMs negotiations is likely to build on the precedents set out in the U.S.-Canada FTA. FTA obligations on performance requirements—which go beyond existing GATT practice as elaborated in the 1983 panel report on the Canadian Foreign Investment

Review Agency—and FTA coverage of practices by states and provinces could provide useful precedents for a GATT accord.

Conclusion

The United States was the driving force behind the creation of the GATT, and it remains today the leading proponent of a strengthened GATT trading system. The United States has been the *demandeur* of all eight rounds of GATT negotiations. No other country has made as great a commitment nor taken as much responsibility for the pursuit of multilateral trade liberalization in the postwar era. These facts should be kept well in mind before one criticizes too sharply the U.S. drift toward protectionism and bilateralism.

From the onset, however, U.S. support for the GATT has been tempered by political pressures to safeguard domestic farm programs and by the reluctance to cede too much enforcement authority to multilateral processes. Efforts to liberalize trade barriers and to expand the coverage of GATT disciplines have proceeded in lock-step with the maintenance of the section 22 waiver and the furtherance of extra-GATT "voluntary" export restraints. Clearly, this "Jekyll and Hyde" approach to the GATT has contributed to the weaknesses in GATT rules and institutional procedures that currently are subject of negotiations in the Uruguay Round.

In some respects, the U.S. approach to the GATT has been surprisingly consistent. It has long noted the importance of considering trade policy in the context of overall economic policy—both at the outset of the postwar era, when it was the predominant global economic power, and today, when economic hegemony is more diverse. In this regard, it has long recognized that global trading rules need to encompass the trade-related aspects of services, investment, and restrictive business practices. It also has been concerned since the 1940s that GATT safeguards rules, especially for BOP purposes, would provide a rationale for long-term protectionism and an exemption from GATT liberalization efforts.[18] Finally, it has long promoted the elaboration of GATT obligations regarding nontariff barriers and the strengthening of GATT dispute settlement procedures to reinforce the foundation of the GATT trading system.

On the other hand, U.S. consistency on its agricultural quotas and on the MFA have worked at cross purposes to the goals noted above. The durability of these quotas and the willingness of the U.S. and other governments to go outside the GATT system to negotiate voluntary export restraints have contributed importantly to the erosion of GATT discipline over the past two decades. Some consistency is a good thing, but, in an interdependent world, countries must adjust to changing competitive forces in world markets.

The future of the GATT depends on the United States and other major trading countries recognizing this adjustment prerequisite, and taking the hard first steps to dismantle over time their longstanding trade barriers. The Uruguay Round provides a true test of their willingness to do so. The future strength and vitality of the multilateral trading system lies in the balance.

Notes

1. During the period 1934 to 1945, the United States entered into 32 bilateral trade agreements under this authority (Jackson 1969, 37).

2. The following paragraphs draw heavily on the insightful analyses of Diebold (1952), Wilcox (1949), and Jackson (1969).

3. Interestingly, only a few years earlier, the run-up to the ITO negotiations was nurtured during the U.S.-British meetings on lend-lease assistance.

4. Indeed, these fears have been realized. Because of lax GATT discipline, most controls notified under the BOP safeguards of GATT Article XVIII have been in place for more than 20 years.

5. In many instances, the threat of antidumping actions has also prompted VERs as well as export price adjustments.

6. However, the danger of retaliation run amok as in the 1930s is highly exaggerated. Retaliation has been used effectively in recent years as a measured response to the imposition of new trade restraints. In this regard, retaliation can bolster the credibility of the trading system by demonstrating that rights under trade agreements can be protected.

7. The Omnibus Trade and Competitiveness Act of 1988 expands this list even further by including export targeting, the abuse of workers' rights, and toleration of cartels as practices actionable under section 301.

8. In the semiconductor case, the United States set a de facto minimum import price, increased tariffs on about $300 million of Japanese imports, and sought market-sharing commitments for U.S. firms in the Japanese market. GATT rules and procedures were short circuited. Indeed, the train of events sparked complaints by the EC against the terms of the original U.S./Japan agreement and by Japan against the U.S. retaliation.

9. For an analysis of the results of the 1982 GATT Ministerial, see Schott (1983). For the Congressional reaction, see Destler (1986, 77ff.).

10. Proponents of such an approach recognize that trade policy measures alone cannot contribute much to solving the trade deficit problem, but that open markets for U.S. exports are a necessary condition for an orderly adjustment of the U.S. current account imbalance. See Bergsten (1988), especially chapter 6.

11. These issues are analyzed in detail in Jeffrey J. Schott, *More Free Trade Areas?*, Policy Analyses in International Economics 27, Washington: Institute for International Economics, May 1989.

12. In September 1988, the U.S. International Trade Commission released a study on a prospective U.S.-Japan FTA, which was originally suggested by Ambassador Mansfield in late 1987.

13. For the most definitive exposition of U.S. policies and strategies on services, see Feketekuty (1988).

14. However, the failure of the United States to change policies which have been found to contravene GATT rules (e.g., DISC) has at times hampered U.S. efforts to pursue this goal.

15. I.M. Destler has noted how these factors undercut domestic support for the GATT: "Furthermore the international trade regime was viewed as ineffective and riddled with exceptions, the less credible was any claim that U.S. interests were served by following the rules that remained" (Destler 1986, 49).

16. One wonders whether U.S. negotiators even relish the threat that existing rules could unravel under such an approach, as it would appease the Code's harsh critics in the Congress.

17. Proposals in these areas are put forward in Hufbauer and Schott (1985), Bergsten et al. (1987), and Cline (1987).

18. I do not mean to be sanctimonious on this last point. The United States also has used or bent GATT rules to protect key sectors of its economy. But in most instances, the channels employed were opened up long before the ITO and GATT were concluded.

References

Baker, James A. III. 1988. "The Geopolitical Implications of the U.S.-Canada Trade Pact." *The International Economy*, January/February.

Bergsten, C. Fred. 1988. *America in the World Economy: A Strategy for the 1990s.* Washington: Institute for International Economics.

Bergsten, C. Fred, Kimberly Ann Elliott, Jeffrey J. Schott, and Wendy E. Takacs. 1987. *Auction Quotas and United States Trade Policy.* Policy Analyses in International Economics 19. Washington: Institute for International Economics, September.

Brock, William E. 1982. "A Simple Plan for Negotiating Trade in Services." *The World Economy*, November.

Cline, William R. 1987. *The Future of World Trade in Textiles and Apparel.* Washington: Institute for International Economics.

Diebold, William Jr. 1952. "The End of the I.T.O." Essays in International Finance 16. International Finance Section, Princeton University. Princeton, New Jersey. October.

Diebold, William Jr. ed. 1988. *Bilateralism, Multilateralism, and Canada in US Trade Policy.* Cambridge, Mass.: Ballinger for the Council on Foreign Relations.

Destler, I.M. 1986. *American Trade Politics: System under Stress.* Washington: Institute for International Economics and New York: Twentieth Century Fund.

Feketekuty, Geza. 1988. *International Trade in Services: An Overview and Blueprint for Negotiations.* Cambridge, Mass.: Ballinger for the American Enterprise Institute.

Hathaway, Dale E. 1987. *Agriculture and the GATT: Rewriting the Rules.* Policy Analyses in International Economics 20. Washington: Institute for International Economics, September.

Horlick, Gary N., Geoffrey D. Oliver, and Debra P. Steger. 1988. "Dispute Resolution Mechanisms." In Schott and Smith (1988).

Hufbauer, Gary Clyde, and Jeffrey J. Schott. 1985. *Trading for Growth: The Next Round of Trade Negotiations.* Policy Analyses in International Economics 11. Washington: Institute for International Economics, September.

Jackson, John H. 1969. *World Trade and the Law of GATT.* Indianapolis: Bobbs-Merrill.

Leutwiler, Fritz, et al. 1985. *Trade Policies for a Better Future: Proposals for Action.* Geneva: GATT Independent Study Group, March.

Reforming World Agricultural Trade. 1988. A Policy Statement by 29 Professionals from 17 Countries. Washington: Institute for International Economics, May.

Schott, Jeffrey J. 1989. *More Free Trade Areas?* Policy Analyses in International Economics 27. Washington: Institute for International Economics, May.

Schott, Jeffrey J. 1988. *United States–Canada Free Trade: An Evaluation of the Agreement.* Policy Analyses in International Economics 24. Washington: Institute for International Economics, April.

Schott, Jeffrey J. 1983. "The GATT Ministerial: A Postmortem." *Challenge,* May/June.

Schott, Jeffrey J., and Jacqueline Mazza. 1986. "Trade in Services and Developing Countries." *Journal of World Trade Law,* May/June.

Schott, Jeffrey J., and Murray G. Smith, eds. 1988. *The Canada–United States Free Trade Agreement: The Global Impact.* Washington: Institute for International Economics.

Snape, Richard H. 1986. *Should Australia Seek a Trade Agreement with the United States?* Economic Planning Advisory Council and the Department of Trade, Discussion Papers no. 86/01, Canberra, June.

Wilcox, Clair. 1949. *A Charter for World Trade.* New York: MacMillan.

4

Japan in the GATT

Hiroshi Kitamura

This chapter addresses the twin issues of GATT reforms and of the broad prospects for the international trading system, mainly from the vantage point of recent international conflicts in which Japan has played a major role. Though it is extensively based on the views prevailing in influential Japanese circles, including the mass media, this chapter does not claim to take a position that could be equated with that of the Japanese government. The author is in no position to identify what the official policy is.

Section 1 deals with the present condition of the international trading system, to which decay of the GATT rules has led. Japan has played a very special role in the development of GATT; this is the subject of Section 2. In evaluating several of the factors that contributed to the erosion of the GATT rules, Section 3 comes to the conclusion that the greatest danger confronting the international trading system stems from bilateral pressures to resolve international trade conflicts. These bilateral pressures threaten the very principle of multilateralism. Finally, Section 4 addresses realistic ways of strengthening the GATT regime.

Erosion of the GATT Rules

How we judge the effectiveness of the postwar international trading system depends on what we regard as the essential requirements and as the ideal image of such a multilateral system. When one recalls GATT's uneasy beginnings as the remnant of what had been envisioned as a body called the International Trade Organization, or ITO, one cannot but regard the early postwar days of GATT as a success story: over the years, surmounting many a crisis, the regime has managed not only to survive but also to expand, organizing several major rounds of trade negotiations, one more extensive than the other. At least until the early

1970s, world trade expanded much faster than world production, leading to an ever-increasing degree of economic interdependence and interaction between nations. An effective tradition of international cooperation, which has proved successful in sparing the world the worst kind of trade wars and trade disintegration, has emerged around the forums of the GATT.

If, however, one chooses to place the emphasis on some elements of the free trade postulate, which should have been the guiding principle of nondiscrimination inherent in the postwar trading rules, ensuring stability and predictability of international transactions, then one will come to quite a different conclusion. In the postwar period, free trade was far from being the norm, as, in the 1950s, agriculture, through a series of waivers and other clauses, had already been exempted from GATT rules. This trend has by no means been arrested, much less reversed, as over the following three decades one sector after the other has been taken out of the GATT orbit into the dictate of managed trade: textiles and clothing, shipbuilding, automobiles, machine tools and electronics. The use of tariffs has declined as a means to reduce imports, and, contrary to GATT's recommendations, nations have resorted to measures like VERs (Voluntary Export Restraints) or OMAs (Orderly Market Agreements) in order to circumvent GATT strictures. Thus, we cannot but draw the conclusion that the postwar multilateral trading system has reached a fairly hopeless stage of advanced decay.

I think that a comprehensive and objective evaluation of the GATT system must comprise both these positive and these negative aspects. And I submit that this will definitely contribute a great deal to a revision of the usual identification of the postwar multilateral trading system with some kind of free trade system. It is worth noting that the "end of laissez faire" (Keynes) was already behind us as the world embarked on sketching a blueprint for the postwar economic order. While the stillborn ITO aimed at regulating restrictive business practices and foreign investment in a positive manner, and at achieving a minimum degree of stability in primary commodity prices, one of the objectives of the General Agreement on Tariffs and Trade, or GATT, is to strive for domestic full employment, which may overrule the principle of freedom of trade. The phrase "embedded liberalism" was coined by Gerald Ruggie in 1982 to designate the prevailing thinking on the desirable international order. "Liberalism was 'embedded' in the acceptance of an extensive role for the state, both in steering the economy and in ensuring a decent life to citizens. Internationally, the form of liberalism agreed to after World War II had to be consistent with the welfare state rather than in conflict with it. Thus, the constraints imposed on national economic policies by the classical gold standard were relaxed, and the pursuit of 'free trade' was replaced by the goal of nondiscrimination. Furthermore, the goal of price stability was sacrificed when this seemed necessary to maintain an open international economy" (Keohane 1984, 19).

I believe that Robert Baldwin was correct when he remarked that emphasis in the GATT was on producers' interests rather than on consumers', as the economic theory of maximization of consumers' welfare would have suggested. This is precisely why, in the postwar period, GATT has been so successful in organizing international cooperation around its forums: producers were primarily interested in expanding their export markets and in achieving maximal economic growth. Contrary to the tenets of the economic theory of free trade, imports were regarded as necessary costs, "concessions," to finance export trade. Thus, unilateral liberalization of trade was precluded as a policy recipe; reduction of barriers to imports had to be negotiated on a "reciprocal" basis, as trade "concessions" by the trading partner were regarded as a necessary precondition for one's own "concessions." The "mercantilist" attitude inherent in the principle of "reciprocity" in tariff negotiations was nothing but a reflection of the GATT bias in favor of producers' interests.

GATT has often been accused of having a dual personality. But, after all, wasn't the agreement the product of a compromise between diverse national and ideological interests? While the principles of multilateralism and tariff reductions were affirmed, so were safeguards, exemptions, exceptions and restrictions—all designed to protect the respective balances of payments as well as a variety of domestic social policies. GATT was thus a typical product of compromises, reflecting the embedded liberalism of the time: "Unlike the economic nationalism of the thirties, it would be multilateral in character; unlike the liberalism of the gold standard and free trade, its multilateralism would be predicated upon domestic interventionism" (Ruggie 1982, 393).

The optimum balance between the two conflicting tendencies in the embedded liberalism depends on the general trends of the economy in the particular phases of long cycles. So long as the economy followed upward trends, as in the 1950s and 1960s, the multilateral aspect of the system was dominant, leading to increasing trade liberalization and integration. The embedded liberalism of the world economy has now come under heavy pressure. Against the background of the economic crises of the 1970s and 1980s, the challenge of Japan and the NIEs began to generate a powerful counterreaction. Increasing state intervention and protectionism, designed at first to cushion societies from some of the adverse effects of economic interdependence, now threatened to undermine liberalism itself. Since they themselves were the fruits of successful world integration, the large-scale shift of production centers from the traditional Atlantic to the periphery of international capitalism and the turn of the terms of trade against the industrialized countries of the West had to cause "defensive" or "contingent" protectionism in these countries to increase to the point of overwhelming the very framework of multilateralism. This is what has become known as "crisis of embedded liberalism."

The challenge GATT is now facing must be viewed in that context. To the extent that government responsibility for domestic social stability is built in the postwar system, GATT as an international organization has proven flexible enough to accommodate changes in international competitiveness and emerging new patterns of comparative advantage. As will be argued below, this is the source of GATT's strength as well as of the weakness of its system of rules. This internal flexibility has enabled GATT to maintain its effectiveness, even in the face of an extensive measure of government protection, so long as the principle of liberalism kept the international trading system sufficiently open. As the further extension of protectionism begins to undermine the openness of the multilateral system, however, GATT will find itself in a crisis. Today, we have come dangerously close to such a threshold of tolerance.

The Problem of Accommodating Japan into the GATT System

In the postwar period, the GATT system has been confronted with very special problems in trying to accommodate Japan, this dynamic and challenging nation, into its own framework. We feel that the problems connected with these historic efforts deserve special attention, for they happen to throw some light on the structural weakness of the system as well as on its strength, i.e., its flexibility in adapting its rules to cope with rapid changes in trade patterns. In fact, Japan's special position in the postwar development of the GATT system is so outstanding that the foremost GATT experts, Gerard Curzon and Victoria Curzon Price, chose this aspect as an organizing principle of their monumental analysis of GATT's history (Gerard Curzon and Victoria Curzon Price 1976, 253–280).

When Japan applied for GATT membership after World War II, memories of the interwar period were still fresh. Whether rightly or wrongly, the Japanese penetration of the world market gave rise then to worldwide charges of social or currency dumpings. The spectacular advances in exports of cheap Japanese goods were seen variously as the result of an enforced post-1931 devaluation of the yen, of cheap labor and other "unfair" trading practices. This was admittedly something more to add to the recent wartime experience with Japan, and in marked contrast to the favorable and expeditious way the Contracting Parties handled the membership applications of Italy and West Germany and admitted them to the GATT, they were seemingly in no mood to offer Japan the same treatment and accept it immediately as a full member. Japan had to wait a full three years before it could formally accede to the GATT. But even then, Japan's accession was made conditional on the invocation against this country of Article XXXV by 14 contracting parties out of a total membership of 38, or 40 percent of Japan's world trade at the time. In the past, only one country, Japan, has had the "distinction" of seeing Article XXXV invoked against it. This article excused the invoking countries from applying GATT rules to a "contracting party" for as long as they wished.

In addition to these 14 countries, almost all of those which did not invoke Article XXXV against Japan did apply quantitative restrictions in a discriminating manner against this country, on grounds of balance of payments difficulties. Thus, it was extremely doubtful that Japan's formal accession to the GATT would bring it any material advantage in terms of GATT rights. For, as long as Japan was in the "dollar zone," the potential for trade discrimination against this country remained virtually unchanged, as compared with the situation before its accession to the GATT.

As by 1964, changes in the international economic environment necessitated the removal of Article XXXV, most West European countries succeeded in converting invocation of Article XXXV not only into discriminatory quotas (as in the case of "noninvoking" countries) but also into a newly invented and officially sanctioned technique of using export restraints as an alternative to import restrictions. In its negotiations of a treaty of commerce, establishment and navigation with Britain, for example, Japan had to agree to limit by means of "voluntary" export control those items which had been limited in the past by unilateral British quotas, and even to "refrain from bringing the matter up in GATT if Britain was ever obliged to return to (discriminatory) quota restrictions," violating the most-favored-nation provisions of the treaty (Gerard Curzon and Victoria Curzon Price 1976, 265).

The fact that even today a series of trade agreements involving safeguard clauses of a discriminatory nature "as between sources of supply" remain in force between most West European countries and Japan is the historical legacy of that period. To the extent that GATT's fundamental principle is that of nondiscrimination, or that of unconditional Most Favored Nation treatment, these clauses, which specifically discriminate against the Japanese sources of supply, are obviously in conflict with the spirit of the GATT system. Also, they would seem to justify Patterson's judgment that they constitute "the most unsavory chapter" in the postwar history of the international trading system. That Japan's negotiating efforts, aimed at the withdrawal of these unilateral discriminatory clauses, have not succeeded as yet has something to do with the problem of identifying the "right" negotiators on the other side, as the West Europeans apparently are not yet sure whether negotiating commercial treaties is the sole responsibility of the European Community as a whole or whether the sovereign EC member countries should be consulted on an individual basis when trying to reach international accords.

In fact, Japan is now about to initiate bilateral trade negotiations with the European Commission, designating the treatment of a total of 89 Japanese products by eleven European countries except Britain—41 in Spain, 36 in Italy, 23 in Portugal and 17 in France—as violating GATT rules. The treatment of the following products by the following EC countries will be more particularly scrutinized: automobiles in Italy, TV sets and radios in France, motorcycles in Spain and machine tools in Portugal. If no bilateral agreement can be reached, the Japanese government will reportedly seek settlement in the GATT forums, under GATT rules. Whether the European Commission or individual West European countries will be able to ignore much longer Japan's legitimate grievances by pointing to the constitutional questions arising in the process of integration is to be doubted.

In 1960, the concept of market disruption was formulated by a so-called "GATT Working Party," providing the basis on which a short-term agreement, or STA, was reached for cotton textiles in 1961, superseded by a long-term arrangement, or LTA, for International Trade in Cotton Textiles in 1962, and finally absorbed into an arrangement for International Trade in Textiles (WTA)—better known as the Multifibre Arrangement, or MFA—in 1973, with several extensions since then. Again, it was Japan which, as the black sheep in the business of trade, became the United States' target of choice in this country's first attempt to have "sensitive" exports "voluntarily" restrained by the exporting nation itself. Since the MFA went into effect, there has been a dramatic increase in the number of exporters and importers participating in it, as well as in that of products covered by it. This has made the MFA in its present form "the apotheosis of the concept of managed trade" (Wolf 1983, 455). The textile arrangements, which marked important phases of Japan's integration into the GATT system, have brought about drastic changes in the nature of the international trading system, whereby the use of export restraints as an alternative to import restrictions has been officially sanctioned by GATT.

But what do these systemic changes actually entail? The United States and other industrial countries have proven reluctant to adapt to the new situation of comparative advantage arising from Japanese competition and that of developing countries. However, the use of Article XIX, the official safeguard clause, would have been cumbersome, entailing "expensive" renegotiations and excluding a discriminatory approach to the source of the disturbance. Just by bringing their overwhelming bargaining power to bear, the importing nations could pressure the exporting ones into "voluntarily" restraining their exports, thereby achieving the same results as through unilateral export restrictions, circumventing the GATT stricture and leaving the exporters somewhat wider discretionary room. As ambiguities were slipped into the GATT, the open multilateral system was transformed into a discriminatory system of sectoral restraints. In the end, what is really involved is the objection to the principle of comparative advantage itself (Wolf 1987, 256).

A look at MFA's history of successive extensions and other renewals clearly shows that the system of sectoral restraints has become increasingly restrictive and complex. About ten years ago, the attempt was made "to impose global ceilings on aggregate imports from 'low-cost' suppliers of certain sensitive products under the doctrine of 'cumulative market disruption' " (Wolf 1983, 459). This did not preclude, however, that "not only were some of the most important suppliers not restricted, but, more striking still, while countries like the United States, Italy or Switzerland faced no restrictions in industrial country markets, developing countries with negligible exports by comparison, like Sri Lanka or Thailand, did" (Wolf 1983, 469–470). All of this means that, most probably, imports into industrialized countries have been diverted from poorer to richer countries.

The attempt to restrain aggregate imports from "low-cost" suppliers of sensitive products would lead to a denial of the necessary historic development of the patterns of international trade. While the first "grayfield" arrangement was advocated by the United States as an importing nation and supported by Japan as an exporting nation, both have now reversed field, the former to protect its interests as an exporter of some capital-intensive textiles and the latter to safeguard its domestic market against increasing imports of knit products from South Korea. In September 1988, in order to reduce the annual growth in textile imports from the present 3 percent to less than 1 percent, the U.S. Senate passed the protectionist "1988 Textile and Apparel Trade Act." While Japan was inclined to protest this U.S. move, its own MITI was trying to persuade South Korea to restrain its exports of knit goods to Japan from July 1988 onward. In fact, South Korean exports of such goods to Japan increased by 29 percent in July 1988 over against the same month of the previous year.

Economic theory holds that the lower the production costs of "low-cost" suppliers are, the greater their gains from trade will be. But producers' interests prevalent in the GATT system dictate that aggregate imports from "low-cost" suppliers be restrained as a matter of policy, which is in obvious and direct conflict with the theory. This is precisely what is involved in the denial of the principle of comparative advantage underlying the political claim that the particular industrial structures of the past must be maintained or that adjustment to the new constellation of comparative advantage must be resisted. This reluctance to adjust is the basic motivation behind the prevailing and growing tendencies toward trade protectionism and state interventionism. Guided by this motivation, GATT faces the risk of being effectively transformed into a sectoral system of discriminatory trade restraints, a far cry from the original idea of a system for multilateral trade expansion.

The refusal to adjust may have far-reaching implications for the long-term prospects of an international trading system. Gerard Curzon and Victoria Curzon Price have pointed to the fact that a viewpoint similar to the "pauper-labor argument" was making the rounds in some influential quarters in advanced industrial countries. The logical long-term consequence of this would be that "Japan could not expect equal treatment until its standard of living approached the developed country norm" (Gerard Curzon and Victoria Curzon Price 1976, 254). This means that an open non-discriminatory trading system is not conceivable between countries with different standards of living, i.e., between the advanced industrial countries of the North and the developing countries of the South. The developing countries must be characterized by a lower standard of real wages, corresponding to an overall lower capital-labor ratio, and the comparative advantage that accrues to the labor-intensive production in developing countries reflects precisely the motive power leading to higher stages of economic development through capital accumulation. This essential mechanism of economic development is now being denied by the so-called "pauper-labor argument," which serves to justify restrictions of imports from "low-cost" countries with lower standards of living.

Threats to Multilateralism

Viewed from the perspective of "embedded liberalism," the crisis of the GATT system is above all a crisis of the open multilateral trading system. It is not the economic role of the state itself that undermines the openness of the system; rather, it is the use of a certain kind of government directive that threatens to shut down the multilateral system. The state may pursue its own objective by organizing state trading, that is, by exporting and importing on government-defined terms of transaction (Kostecki 1982, 22), and yet maintain the principle of liberalism in world trade. Also, the existence of centrally planned economies is compatible with the multilateral nature of their trade relations, as long as their import and export channels are kept open.

The worst enemy of multilateralism, however, is bilateralism, or yet imperialism, as an instrument of economic warfare. Those nations which resort to bilateral pressures to achieve political purposes of their own would hardly qualify for integration into a multilateral system, as such a policy tends to divide the world into competing blocs. And the tendency toward a system of sectoral restraints on trade, which originated with agriculture, textiles and clothing, is spreading rapidly to other sectors. Today, it is the greatest danger facing the open multilateral system, as the degree of discrimination inherent in it threatens to undermine the principle of multilateralism. A certain degree of discrimination always accompanies the necessary intervention of states in economic affairs. In cases of scattered intervention, such discrimination may still be compatible with the open character of the multilateral system. In a system of sectoral "gray-field" restrictions, however, discrimination tends to exceed the threshold of tolerance, thus making the very principle of liberalism all but applicable.

The danger of bilateralism and "sectoralism" for multilateralism has been brought into sharp focus by the wave of reciprocity legislation enacted by the U.S. Congress at the beginning of the 1980s. In the second half of the preceding decade, a radical change took place in the way reciprocity was conceptualized. Originally, the concept of reciprocity (in the sense of equality in tariff concessions, i.e., in changes in tariffs), which stems from the Cordell Hull trade legislation, had been used in the procedures of GATT's tariff negotiations. That it was criticized by liberals as reflecting mercantilist attitudes has been mentioned earlier. By contrast, what is sought by the new concept is equality in the levels of protection, that is, in the levels of market access, on a bilateral as well as sectoral basis. This concept goes far beyond the basic principle of national treatment, as in the traditional free trade postulate. Equality would now mean that institutions of different nations can be compared with one another, or that a strong nation should have the right to complain about a lack of harmonization in the social and institutional conditions of a weak nation. Earlier, the absence of state intervention was supposed to result in foreign firms being treated just like one's national firms. Focusing on the fact that access to foreign markets for one's national firms may vary from country to country, reciprocity now would require foreign firms in one country's market to be treated the same way as that country's firms in the foreign firms' home market.

To be sure, this new concept has opened up the possibility of retaliation and trade wars, for aggressive reciprocity enforced by retaliation threatens

"U.S. retaliation in the form of higher protection against any foreign country that does not grant comparable market access to U.S. exports" (Cline 1983, 121). The natural, if not necessarily rational, response to such U.S. retaliatory measures can only be stepped up retaliation on the part of the United States' trading partners. And the negotiating attitude of aggressive reciprocity does not only put more teeth into the U.S. Omnibus Trade and Competitiveness Act of 1988; it is also bound to influence some essential aspects of the future commercial policy of the European Community, for example, in the field of financial liberalization. Also of relevance to the context of the present discussion is the fact that the negotiations on the new principle of reciprocity threaten to find their way into some GATT forums.

This could have far-reaching consequences because "a move to a policy of attempting to force foreign liberalization through the threat of retaliation would almost inevitably violate the principle of unconditional most-favored-nation treatment that has been the foundation of trade negotiations for decades . . ." (Cline 1983, 131).

There are divergent views as to whether a conditional application of the principle of nondiscrimination would lead by itself to a breakdown of the multilateral trading system. Of course, the general view tends to emphasize the importance of the unconditional application of the MFN principle for the unprecedented expansion of world trade in the postwar period, but deviation from it has long been permitted by special exceptions in the General Agreement for specific regional integration schemes and for government procurement. It was even possible to argue that the original conceptualization of GATT's principle of nondiscrimination was based on a conditional application, as it was considered applicable only to GATT signatories.

In recent years, the tendency toward conditional nondiscrimination has become even more apparent. The Generalized System of Preferences, or GSP, for the developing countries was a major departure from the MFN principle. So is the proposed new "United States Caribbean Basin Initiative," or CBI. Also, only those countries which signed the NTB codes of the Tokyo Round are allowed to benefit from them, especially from those on subsidies and government procurement. Even in the context of GATT reforms, the question of compatibility of conditional nondiscrimination with the functioning of the multilateral system has been extensively discussed, and significant attempts have been made to minimize the destructive effects of conditional MFN being accepted as the necessary price to be paid for a legalistic tightening of multilateral trade discipline. It has even been argued that the principle of multilateralism should replace the traditional function of the MFN principle in maintaining the effectiveness of a multilateral trading system (Jan Tumlir). Although the Contracting Parties will have to face the issue of conditional or unconditional MFN squarely sooner or later, there is no doubt that, at the present juncture, the bulk of world trade is governed by the traditional GATT interpretation of MFN clauses, thus allowing the multilateral trading system to function in rough outlines.

As William R. Cline emphasized, however, the recent U.S. reciprocity policies mark a more fundamental departure from the MFN principle than previous GATT practices. While the NTB codes of the Tokyo Round were "multilateral and trade-creating in nature" (Cline 1983, 136), the new U.S. policy, based on the new concept of reciprocity to the contrary, would be "bilateral in nature" and would "more often result in trade suppression rather than trade creation" (Cline, ibid.).

In short, a very deadly weapon has now been forged by the leading member of the postwar international trading system, which hitherto has made decisive contributions to the viability of the multilateral system. Thus, in its current crisis, the GATT system is endangered by bilateralism and "sectoralism," which, buttressed by the reciprocity policy of enforced retaliation, threaten to undermine its underlying principle of multilateralism. The general approach to conflict management in GATT, which suggests several ways and means for achieving reforms, must now be examined in order to see the practical relevance of these threats to the multilateral GATT system.

GATT Reforms: Toward an Effective Multilateral System

This is not the place to look in detail at all the proposals that have been made in the past for strengthening the trade discipline of the GATT system in order to ensure system-conforming actions by all countries and secure predictability of the system as well as transparency of policy measures. We will thus concern ourselves with the broad approaches to reforms of the GATT system in order to conclude our exposition on the threats to multilateralism.

One may start from the assumption that GATT is a juridical system which embodies not only the rule of law but also the enforcement of it at the international level. Then, one wishes to extend the current perfect rules to new sectors such as services and investment. Provided loopholes have been found in this system of law, for example, with regard to subsidies and dumping, they must be eliminated; the most convenient way to do it is through proceedings on settlement of trade disputes. This somewhat legalistic approach underlies much of the U.S. policy on GATT reforms. And it has also led to an uninterrupted series of American complaints that other countries have violated the GATT rules. Not only is GATT in no position to decide who is right and who is wrong, but it does not impose sanctions itself. The truth of the matter is that "the GATT itself is really not a juridical system, nor is it an enforcement body." "The GATT is not a court," charged with authoritative interpretation of the system of law. "It is a system of balanced rights and obligations, together with a cumulation of trade agreements based on mutual concessions and on national decisions to agree, or not agree, with other nations" (Malmgren 1983, 193).

Any international organization provides a mechanism designed to resolve disputes between nations in the light of the rules incorporated in international agreements. Although GATT procedures for settling trade disputes proved formally rather effective, most problems have arisen, in the judgment of a competent observer, "from disagreements over, and imbalances in, certain substantive GATT legal disciplines" (Petersmann 1988, 69) such as those dealing with subsidies. This means that unless agreement can be reached in making GATT rules more precise, and until GATT's legal disciplines are made more balanced—for example, by terminating "waivers" granted to only certain contracting parties— GATT rules cannot be regarded as perfect rules, worthy of the respect of all member countries.

In fact, GATT has soft and loose rules, riddled with exceptions and loopholes. GATT is the cumulative effect of negotiations—negotiated general philosophy and rules, combined with specifically negotiated trade concessions. As it lacks a theory, GATT does not aim at a straightforward realization of some kind of optimum world structure, as, for example, the maximization of people's welfare; it is rather a negotiated agreement whereby policy objectives and aspirations of different nations are harmonized to some extent. GATT is thought of as providing only a forum for international meetings and a framework for international cooperation. For instance, since every nation today implicitly subsidizes its domestic production or its exports, GATT has had great difficulty in arriving at an agreement on a permissible level of subsidies.

The choice before the negotiating nations is: either GATT can point the way toward harmonization at lower levels by restraining subsidies, or disadvantaged countries, on their own initiative, will harmonize trade practices at higher levels of intervention by introducing new subsidies (Hufbauer 1984, 180). This pragmatic approach, which aims at achieving harmony and agreement rather than insisting on principles, seems to dominate the present situation. The result may not be the best in theory, but may be the best that is possible (Corden 1983, 745).

Provided attention can be focused on how differences or conflicts about the interpretation of GATT rules are actually dealt with and settled at the present juncture, it then will be possible to devise and implement concrete action programs to enhance the effectiveness of the GATT system. Since GATT was not originally intended to serve as an international organization but had no other choice than to step into this role following the ITO's stillbirth, its internal structure was, and still is, all but solid. The same is true of its dispute-settlement provisions—they were, and to a degree still are, weak, sketchy and rather ambiguous. Their history is one of improvising on the extremely inadequate language of Article XXIII, which deals with remedies for "nullification or impairment" of negotiated liberalization commitments, and in the course of which occasionally established working parties were gradually replaced by panels to help contracting parties come to decisions. But the current GATT procedures for dispute settlement are not effective enough to make the GATT body a working juridical system. "There is a certain amount of ambiguity at almost every step of this procedure. Furthermore, there are ample opportunities for delay. (Most) unfortunately, it is not clear what the legal result of a panel finding is. It appears that there is no legal obligation to carry out a panel finding, at least until the GATT contracting parties approve the panel reports, and even then there has been considerable ambiguity" (Jackson 1983, 181). In fact, it appears, as in the case of Australia's complaint against the EC on sugar, that an economically powerful country can indefinitely resist a panel finding and render the whole procedure a nullity (Teese 1982, 45). Such legal incompetence cannot but have a devastating effect on the confidence of economically weak small and midsize countries in the multilateral trading system.

Harald B. Malmgren, a former U.S. trade negotiator, has come out with a critical analysis of big power behavior in the GATT forums, from which we would like to quote rather extensively: "The U.S. and the EEC tend to dominate the GATT proceedings. . . . They have both ignored GATT decisions when its opinions have been uncomfortable (for example the EEC on sugar, and the U.S. in relation to Domestic International Sales Corporation, DISC). Lately the EEC and the United States have abused the GATT process by bringing poorly defined, conceptually unsound complaints. The broad Article XXIII complaint brought by the EEC against virtually the whole of Japan, Inc. and the recent spate of U.S. agricultural subsidy complaints, based on a weak interpretation of the Multilateral Trade Negotiations (MTN) subsidies code, are examples of this tendency to use the GATT selectively as an instrument of national or regional policy. . . ." (Malmgren 1983, 196).

"The fact that the two dominant trading powers often sort out their difficulties privately, and come into the GATT with convergent positions and policies that affect other nations, has undermined the confidence of these other nations in the effectiveness of the GATT system. . . . The tendency of the United States and the European Common Market to pick and choose when and how to use the GATT, and to opt for alternative venues when it suits them; the tendency for the two giants to use their power to coerce other nations to behave in a certain manner, outside the multilateral framework—these are the most serious political and procedural challenges to the viability and effectiveness of the GATT system" (Malmgren 1983, 197–198).

What I would like to stress in this connection is the tendency of the dominant trading powers "to opt for alternative venues when it suits them" (Malmgren, op. cit.). Increasingly, the United States is resorting to a policy of bilateral negotiations to settle trade disputes, at least those in which Japan is involved. As in the face of sharpening competition from Japanese manufacturers of semiconductors the American electronics industry began losing ground, the U.S. negotiating team sought a solution that eventually took the form of a traditional bilateral Orderly Marketing Agreement, or OMA. Signed in August 1986, the so-called Orderly Marketing Agreement for "Sunset" Industries was geared to two types of market operations: the first aimed at raising the offer prices of Japanese semiconductors, both in the United States and in third-country markets while the second was designed to increase the share of U.S. semiconductors in the Japanese market, both taking no account whatsoever of the interests of other producers, the European Community included. As for the first objective, the need to regulate dumping prices soon disappeared as Japan's export prices wound up exceeding the U.S.-determined Fair Market Value (FMV), owing to strict monitoring and restraints on production and investment. But the United States is seemingly unwilling to consider either the withdrawal of the OMA or the lifting of sanctions against Japan, which it justifies by alleged Japanese violations of the terms of the agreement.

EC complaints to the GATT, meanwhile, have led to a GATT panel decision that the price monitoring conducted by the Japanese government was at odds with GATT rules. As for the second objective of the agreement, the panel questioned the legal validity of the Japanese-style "administrative guidance," which has the same effect as an international cartel in that it fixes the market shares of individual firms. Indeed, at the time, the United States was reported to have insisted on a 20 percent share of the Japanese semiconductor market. That all bilateral agreements of the traditional type such as Voluntary Export Restraints (VERs) or Orderly Marketing Agreements (OMAs) contain explicit or implicit clauses of market sharing is well known. But it is also a fact that the market follows its own logic and is not amenable to government dictates. Regardless of whether the U.S.-Japanese agreement on semiconductors can be considered a success or, on the contrary, should be deemed a failure, the EC move showed clearly the limits of a one-sided reliance of Japanese trade policy on the United States. Also, it demonstrated that bilateralism and "sectoralism" do not contribute to making the GATT system a stronger, more effective regime. In this trade conflict, Japan wound up entirely isolated as it came under attack from the Newly Industrialized Economies, or NIEs, and other developing countries, too.

Another recent U.S.-Japanese trade dispute concerned U.S. beef and citrus exports to Japan. Bilateral talks in April and May of 1988 stalled because the United States, owing to its own Meat Import Act, would not agree to Japanese variable import levies while Japan was prepared to shift the discussion to the multilateral forums of the GATT, former U.S. Secretary of State George Shultz intervened personally on May 9, 1989, bringing the talks to a conclusion with his proposal for a variable tariff. If anything, this is but another proof that the United States favors bilateral trade accords—also those reached after application of some behind-the-scenes pressure of its own—over multilateral trade settlements.

Agriculture is now on the agenda of the Uruguay Round of multilateral trade negotiations. Early on, the Japanese government made known its intention to discuss the entire problem of agricultural liberalization in an equitable manner and within the framework of the MTN negotiations, together with the question of waivers granted to U.S. and EC import levies. In this connection, there was a tacit agreement between the United States and Japan that rice should not be made the subject of bilateral negotiations. However, Section 301 of the Trade Act of 1974, as amended in 1979, has now been included in the Omnibus Trade and Competitiveness Act, making it a weapon of the first order in the bilateral trade offensive. In September 1988, the U.S. Rice Millers' Association, or RMA, submitted the United States Representative (USTR) its appeal for invocation of Section 301, demanding that the Japanese open their market to up to one million tons of U.S. rice within four years. Toward the end of October of the same year, the RMA's request was turned down with the understanding that Section 301 would be invoked anew if the prospects for trade liberalization of rice had not brightened by the time of the Uruguay Round midterm review in December 1988. This is yet another indication of the premier role bilateral pressures play in U.S. trade policy vis-à-vis other nations.

In view of the growing and alarming tendency among the powerful trading powers to favor bilateralism and "sectoralism," it is important to stress that a return to the original idea of multilateralism is the best way to secure a more effective multilateral trading system. In the realm of international trade, too, the objective should be to achieve a higher degree of harmonization and cooperation, no less than in the fields of finance and macroeconomic policy. The time might have come for Japan to broaden its concept of trade and hence to pursue a more balanced trade policy, that is, to shift the emphasis of it from the current one-sided dependence on the United States to a greater awareness of the world community, including the neighboring countries of Asia and the distant center of Europe.

References

Cline, William R., " 'Reciprocity': A New Approach to World Trade Policy," in: Cline, William R. (ed.), *Trade Policy in the 1980s*, Washington, D.C., Institute of International Economics, 1983.

Corden, W. Max, "Panel Discussion: Towards a Policy Synthesis," in: Cline, William R. (ed.), *Trade Policy in the 1980s*, Washington, D.C., Institute for International Economics, 1983.

Curzon, Gerard and Victoria, "The Management of Trade Relations in the GATT," in: Shonfield, Andrew (ed.), *International Economic Relations of the Western World 1959–1971*, Vol. I, Politics and Trade, Part II, London, Oxford University Press for the Royal Institute of International Affairs, 1976.

Hufbauer, Gary Clyde and Joanna Shelton Erb, *Subsidies in International Trade*, Washington, D.C., Institute for International Economics, 1984.

Jackson, John H., "GATT Machinery and the Tokyo Round Agreement," in: Cline, William R. (ed.), *Trade Policy in the 1980s*, Washington, D.C., Institute for International Economics, 1983.

Keohane, Robert O., "The World Political Economy and the Crisis of Embedded Liberalism," in: Goldthorpe, John H. (ed.), *Order and Conflict in Contemporary Capitalism*, Oxford, Clarendon Press, 1984.

Kostecki, M. M., "State Trading in Agricultural Products by the Advanced Countries," in: Kostecki, M. M. (ed.), *State Trading in International Markets—Theory and Practice of Industrialized and Developing Countries*, London, Macmillan, 1982.

Malmgren, Harald B., "Threats to the Multilateral System," in: Cline, William R. (ed.), *Trade Policy in the 1980s*, Washington, D.C., Institute for International Economics, 1983.

Petersmann, Ernst-Ulrich, "Strengthening GATT Procedures for Settling Trade Disputes," in: *The World Economy*, Vol. 11, No. 1, March 1988.

Ruggie, John Gerard, "International Regimes, Transactions, and Change: Embedded Liberalism in the Postwar Economic Order," in: *International Organization*, 36, 2, Spring 1982.

Teese, C. F., "A View from the Dress Circle in the Theatre of Trade Disputes," in: *The World Economy*, Vol. 5, Nr. 1, March 1982.

Wolf, Martin, "Fiddling while GATT Burns," in: El-Agraa, Ali M. (ed.), *Protection, Cooperation, Integration and Development*, London, Macmillan, 1987.

Wolf, Martin, "Managed Trade in Practice: Implications of the Textile Arrangements," in: Cline, William R. (ed.), *Trade Policy in the 1980s*, Washington, D.C., Institute for International Economics, 1983.

5

EC and GATT: A European Proposal for Strengthening the GATT Dispute Settlement Procedures

Meinhard Hilf

"Governments may end up having created an effective litigation procedure in spite of themselves."[1]

INTRODUCTION

GATT dispute settlement (DS) is in dispute or even in disrepute.[2] It is like many other forms of international procedures for litigation a constant and increasing source of concerns.[3] Recently a few serious deadlocks in the GATT DS procedures, all in the field of agriculture and especially under the Subsidies Code,[4] were sufficient to discredit the most effective and unique DS system that economic organizations operating on a worldwide basis have ever experienced.

From the very beginning the contracting parties to GATT underlined the *legal character* of the agreed rules by establishing the central DS procedure in Articles XXII and XXIII.[5] This procedure followed the evolution of the GATT Agreement by successive amendments and pragmatical improvements as in 1966, 1979, 1982 and 1984.[6] In view of their reciprocal expectations, the contracting parties shared the basic understanding that trade rules are only of worth if they are applied and if an effective DS procedure is at hand.

The Ministerial Declaration of September 20, 1986, opening the New Round, follows the same line: it would be meaningless to negotiate further rules, if at the end there were no confidence that the new rules would be effectively implemented and applied. Thus the Declaration reads:

In order to ensure prompt and effective resolution of disputes to the benefit of all contracting parties, negotiations shall aim to improve and strengthen the rules and the procedures of the dispute settlement process, while recognizing the contribution that would be made by more effective and enforceable GATT rules and disciplines.[7]

This declaration expresses one common understanding of all contracting parties: the enforceable character of agreed rules depends on an effective DS system and the effectiveness of the DS system depends on the clarity and on the negotiated rules. There is a logical and *reciprocal interdependence* between the quality of legal rules and their enforceability.

John Jackson discussed various issues relating to the definition and quality of "GATT law."[8] Doubts seem to relate to the concept of unlimited national sovereignty according to which matters of vital concern to states cannot be subject to judicial review. Foreign trade relations, being inseparably linked to the internal economic policy, are certainly of such vital concern.

This concept fails to notice that many states have, under their constitutions, learned to live with judicial review over all state activities. This review is expanding in all forms of constitutional systems. Of course, the *danger of a juridification* of politics and also of foreign politics exists. But it is inherent to any system of judicial review that it keeps itself in balance with the legitimate interests of the policy-making institutions. Observing judicial self-restraint courts have in areas of vital public interests exercised a strict control on the given procedures.[9] At the same time the courts have recognized wide political or economic discretion of the responsible institutions. The more technical and complex a specific matter, the more the courts try not to interfere with various forms of consent-settlement by the interested parties. For example, under national law this trend may be observed in the fields of environment, when electrical or atomic power-stations are built, and in the field of antitrust law.[10] Thus in reality the existence of courts with binding jurisdiction very often merely provide a threat and a focus for a negotiated settlement by the parties involved.[11]

This development under national law finds its equivalent increasingly in the international relations between states. The signing of the worldwide Law of the Sea Convention on December 10, 1982, which includes various innovative and flexible forms of binding procedures for dispute settlement including judicial review, is certainly the most recent and prominent example.[12] On the European continent the twelve Member States of the European Community (EC) have referred any dispute among themselves or with the Community's institutions to the binding jurisdiction of the Court of Justice of the European Communities (CJEC).

In Article 219 EEC Treaty Member States agreed not to submit such disputes to any methods of settlement other than those provided for in this Treaty. The mere existence of this Court has helped Member States in nearly all cases under dispute among themselves to find solutions to their conflicts by negotiation and consent. Only in exceptional cases interstate disputes have been submitted to the CJEC.[13]

Turning to the international economic relations of states and for example of the EC, one may ask whether there is, under *constitutional law,* a legal obligation to look for and to agree to the same kind of binding DS arrangements. In national constitutional law it is a much debated subject as to what extent the responsible institutions for the handling of foreign affairs are, at least implicitly, bound to observe the basic constitutional principles in their conduct of foreign political and economic relations.[14] However, no national constitution contains an explicit obligation in this sense.

In regard to GATT two different understandings of agreed DS procedures exist. The positions have ranged from looking at the GATT system as being a purely diplomatic or political system or as constituting a quasi-judicial or more and more legally structured system. In doctrine and practice any opinion between a power or a rule-oriented concept may be found.[15] This is probably due to the different aims of the GATT DS procedures. These do not only tend to secure the fulfillment of agreed rules; they also settle any dispute by diplomatic negotiations when a nullification or impairment of protected economic benefits is in dispute. Apparently, under no national legal system are GATT rules considered to be directly applicable.[16] Does this not reflect the more power-oriented interpretation of the GATT Agreement which leaves wide political discretion to the negotiators, that is, to governmental officials?

What will be the attitude of the main contracting parties as to the future shape of the DS system under GATT? How will and should the system look after the New Round?

From an academic position one is free to speculate. Some aspects will be indicated which, of course, may only scratch the surface. Looking from the European side such speculation has some more solid ground in regard to the attitude of the EC.

The European Community

The EC is said to follow primarily a more power-oriented approach in its international trade relations. Certainly, many declarations and decisions of the European institutions could prove this attitude.[17] Yet from the following few observations a more differentiated view will emerge, especially if one keeps in mind that it is essentially the twelve

Member States which may have different views when formulating the foreign trade policy within the EC Council.

Reasons for a Power-Oriented Attitude of the EC

(1) As has been said, *Member States* still play an important part in the formulation of the foreign policy of the EC. They have different views and interests as to the importance of trade and undistorted competition. Their concept of sovereignty is different.[18] Any more rule-oriented approach would need, in fact, unanimity or at least a broad majority in the EC Council.[19]

(2) Such agreement can better be obtained if the Council only decides to muddle through, to negotiate, and to finally let problems lie in suspense instead of pressing for a clear-cut negotiated solution. From the practice under GATT Frieder Roessler has given some relevant examples.[20] The *international decision-making constraints* within the Council have often hindered clear and timely decisions. According to this view, the specific complexity of the internal decision-making process inside the EC seems to be one of the reasons that the EC has not succeeded in negotiating actively on those sensitive political issues which seem incompatible with GATT rules. On its side the United States (U.S.), already in 1948, has succeeded to negotiate waivers in its favour and has succeeded in getting agreement of its partners on further sensitive issues. The EEC—which never negotiated the basic GATT Agreement of 1948—always preferred to content itself with ad hoc solutions leaving the legal issues in suspense (e.g., preferential agreements with mediterranean countries, conditions under Article XXIV GATT). Thus, the EC is apparently playing a more passive and defensive role in spite of its strong position inside GATT.

(3) The CJEC has consistently denied any direct applicable effects of GATT law within the legal order of the EC.[21] Thus acts of the Council and of the Commission cannot be challenged by individuals on the ground that there may be a violation of GATT law. Of course, the Member States can attack such decisions, but they have not done so.[22]

As a result, the EC institutions may feel free to follow a more power-oriented approach. The established, but not undisputed *doctrine of priority* of public international law over any act of secondary EC law, as it has been stated by the case law of the CJEC,[23] has had only limited effects on the handling of GATT affairs by the EC's institutions. One may even suspect that this assumption of priority of public international law over secondary EC law makes the CJEC hesitant to recognize a direct applicable effect of international treaties. Under the doctrine of priority, the recognition of the direct applicability of a treaty leads to political immobilism on the side of the EC Council, which apparently is feared at present. Only without the rule of priority the Council would be in a position to adopt conflicting regulations as *leges posteriori*, if this would be in the compelling interest of the EC. Curious as it may be, by recognizing the priority of public international law to secondary EC law, the CJEC, in reality, has not favoured the applicability of public international law within the EC. A direct effect is more likely to be attributed to a treaty rule if the EC's institutions were still considered to be free to break the relevant rule of international law, if ever necessary.

(4) A more rule-oriented approach would lead to a *shift of influence from the Member States* to the EC. A strengthening of international DS procedures, even if they were eventually based on consensus, in practice strengthens the position of the national or even the EC executive versus the legislator. In the case of the EC, however, this would also reduce the role and influence of the EC-Member States within the GATT framework. If substantive issues are dealt with in the traditional method, that is by negotiations leading to new rules, the EC Council and thus the Member States decide. In contrast, dispute settlement lies in the hands of the Commission with only a limited participation of national representatives. It is an open question whether this participation is even legally required by EC law.[24]

(5) The EC may *not be forced*, on the basis of its own legislation, to open GATT DS procedures. Until recently there was no similar European act like Section 301 of the U.S. Trade law[25] which could have forced the Commission to resort to the relevant DS procedures under GATT. The parallel so called New Trade Policy Instrument, adopted in September 1984, has until now led only to three private complaints.[26] The hurdles of admissability seem to be too high to expect great pressure on the EC to resort to GATT DS procedures. This, at least, holds for the foreseeable future.

(6) Finally, the EC is certainly among the more *powerful* contracting parties within GATT. Having a strong bargaining position, the EC may not feel dependent on legal protection by any legal procedures. Adding the states associated to the EC gives to the latter a solid majority of votes within the GATT Council. It is not surprising that, until recently, few lawyers have been involved in the representation of the EC in GATT DS procedures.[27]

In conclusion, it is not surprising that the EC has consistently under-scored the necessity of consensus in the DS procedures. It seems to be not without reason that the EC is sensitive and sceptical in regard to the gap-filling and law-creating function of the DS procedure. Especially in regard to the EC, a large number of sensitive questions under GATT have not been settled, as for example the question of subsidies in agriculture.[28]

Reasons for a Rule-Oriented Approach of the EC

(1) EC Member States have learned, as have no other states in the world, to submit some of their vital economic issues to the jurisdiction of a common supranational court, the CJEC. Of course, this is due to the specific conditions of integration, but with every further step into the Common Market the lesson is learned: Without a reliable and enforceable DS procedure any further steps toward economic integration would be vulnerable and would not encourage private business to make long-term investments relying on the Common Market.

(2) This lesson has influenced the EC's institutions in their handling of international relations. In contrast to earlier treaty practice, it is surprising that the EC, particularly in recent years, has begun to accept DS arrangements, including binding arbitration[29] and in one exceptional case even judicial procedures before a permanent court.[30] One can find already some forty international agreements in which the EC has consented to arbitration and other forms of judicial settlement. Especially since the middle of the seventies relevant clauses have been agreed upon. Here one finds a number of cooperation and fisheries agreements as well as agreements in the field of atomic research and cooperation. The same is true for an increasing number of multilateral agreements in the field of environmental protection and, to give the latest example, in the Law of the Sea Convention.[31]

Even in GATT the EC has begun to play a more active role, which to a large extent, but not entirely, seems to be due to the quite natural effect of counter-punching, especially against American activism.[32] The EC is on its way to finding a solid basis for its international personality and to agreeing on firm commitments in its international affairs.[33]

Finally, it does not seem unlikely that the EC could become more open-minded and willing to negotiate a more rule-oriented approach to GATT DS procedures if this would be beneficial and adequate to the kind of economic relations in question and if there is a justifiable expectation that its trading partners will subscribe to and respect corresponding obligations.

United States

The position of the United States as to the present and future shape of the DS procedures under GATT has been, at least until recently, more clear and less sophisticated than that on the European side. The internal decision-making procedures on the United States side are certainly more streamlined, transparent, and effective, though there is a constant quarrel about an excessively cumbersome decision-making process. However this may be, the legislator is more exposed to the influence of pressure groups and to other democratic controls than is the case on the European side.[34] Thus, any prediction as to the future position of the American side is difficult. Still in 1982 official proposals of the United States have favoured a clear, legal-oriented approach. For a nation with powerful economic resources, such a supposed rule-oriented policy is not self-evident.[35]

Recent developments, however, shed some doubt as to the future position of the United States in the forthcoming negotiations. Any proposal for a more stringent DS procedure today would likely meet with more hesitation. This may be due to the final decision of the Case Nicaragua v. U.S. by the International Court of Justice (ICJ) in 1984. This case led to the withdrawal of the United States from the Court's jurisdiction.[36] The Gulf of Maine Arbitral Award, handed down by a chamber of the ICJ, also, has aroused critical comments.[37] The Canadian proposal for a binding arbitration clause in the proposed U.S.-Canadian Free Trade Agreement has, for a moment, raised unfavourable reactions in Congress. It was concluded that binding arbitration on any issue of unfair trade between Canada and the United States would automatically limit the powers to take unilateral actions under the Trade Act.[38] Under a final compromise, both sides agreed to include a procedure for binding arbitration in the final agreement.[39] Thus the two countries followed their long tradition of having bilateral disputes resolved by binding arbitration. Even today, the JAY-Treaty of 1794 is still in force.[40]

There are more indications that would suggest a more reluctant position of the United States:

- American Courts also deny any direct applicability to GATT rules;
- the United States does not trust the GATT-voting process which gives a large majority to the EC (including its associated partners);[41] and
- foreign trade instruments allow the protection of national economic interests by measures which may even be inconsistent with the existing international obligations under GATT.[42]

Consequently a stronger GATT DS procedure would, on the one hand, help the American administration at home to appease pressures from protectionist circles.[43] But given the rule of consensus, it would, on the other hand, not bind the hands of the executive if the protection of national economic interests is at stake.

The position of the United States seems at least to be open.[44] It will be interesting to see to what extent the strong demand for "total justice" under domestic law[45] will in the end also influence the attitude in favour of more effective DS procedures. In a legal system which seems to be characterized by too many laws and lawyers[46] and by general expectations of justice, if not by an obsession with law, any strong backing for a clear rule-oriented approach in the field of foreign trade relations would only be consistent. The supposed litigious character of the American society may have its origin in the general expectations for "total justice" within the modern State.[47]

This "no-risk" attitude is certainly shared by most of those operating in the field of foreign trade. The only question is whether this right and claims consciousness only finds its expression in strong demands for unilateral legal protection by the administration or whether it may be understood that an effective DS procedure within a multilateral context would be in the long run the only beneficial answer to conflicts in trade issues.

Japan

It would be presumptuous to predict the attitude of Japan. By tradition Japan shows an official dislike for any formal DS procedures inside and outside the country. A preference for "Gyosei Shido" (administrative guidance) and negotiated settlement without publicity seems to prevail. But Japan seems to follow more and more modern trends and tends to move from a "consensus-society" to a "conflict-society." Japan has signed the Law of the Sea Convention, thereby indicating that there is not a firm doctrine for or against a more rule-oriented approach if it is in the national interest.[48] Japan seems to be supporting the aim of rendering the GATT DS procedure more effective without, however, aiming at a binding judicial system.[49]

Developing Countries

Of course, there is no identical view on the side of developing countries. But being among the least powerful partners within GATT, it would seem reasonable that these states would favour protection by more legalized procedures since retaliatory powers are not readily available.[50] Developing countries begin to rely more on the system of GATT than on the system of UNCTAD. They may hope to benefit from a more active involvement of the GATT-Secretariat which could offer its good offices.

State-Trading Countries

Even state-trading countries appear to support more effective DS procedures, including judicial elements. The USSR and other state-trading countries have signed the Law of the Sea Convention. At the same time, the government of the USSR and the doctrine signalize a more open approach to judicial forms of settlement of disputes under public international law.[51] Thus the state-trading countries, which are contracting parties to GATT, may have an open attitude.

Summing up, there are prospects for a more positive outcome of the New Round in relation to DS, although drastic changes seem to be excluded.

The purpose of the following is not to propose or design new "super-rules" or ideal structures. First, under a more limited approach, I will reiterate the merits and defaults of the existing system (II). Second, having the list of problems at hand, I will look at DS procedures in other comparable organizations (III). And third, equipped with comparative material, I will discuss a list of possible solutions for the ongoing negotiations (IV). My final conclusions will underscore the view that a more rule-oriented approach is inevitable in an economic environment in which, by necessity, the national economies are becoming more interrelated and interdependent (V).

MERITS AND SHORTCOMINGS OF THE DS PROCEDURES IN GATT

Merits

Since 1948 the DS procedures in the central GATT Agreement and in various side agreements have evolved through understandings and by custom. There are different purposes for the DS procedures. These procedures intend to reach credible and speedy solutions for:

- the realization of the GATT rules;
- the protection of reciprocal benefits;
- the settlement of disputes and
- the prevention of future violations.

An additional purpose of the procedure, but only within confined limits, is to reach new understandings on and adaptations of unclear rules (law—creative function).[52] These are rather diverging aims of the fragmented procedures which are most difficult to reconcile. It is not known how many disputes have developed in relation to GATT obligations and how many disputes have been settled outside the official DS procedures by bilateral negotiations.[53] Contracting parties have formally opened the formalized GATT DS procedures in more than 200 cases, out of which some 100 cases were based on Article XXIII GATT.[54] More than fifty panel reports have been delivered under the central procedure out of which, since 1981, four have not been adopted by the Contracting Parties (CPs). Under the Subsidies Code three other panel reports had, for a long time, failed to be accepted by the CPs.[55] These latter three cases, all in the field of agriculture, are considered to be a decisive blow to the respect for the entire GATT DS system. Still, the increasingly frequent use of the DS procedures signifies a persistent will of the CPs to resolve their disputes by commonly agreed procedures.

The high number of disputes which have been brought before the CPs, and which is still increasing, is certainly one of the merits of the existing system. One may speculate whether this would be the same under a system in which no consensus would be required or in which the CPs would decide without the parties in dispute. A unanimous decision of the CPs is a strong argument for national governments to fend off protectionist tendencies at home. Thus, the rule of consensus and the strong negotiating element in the deliberations of the CPs guarantee a large degree of autonomy to the parties in dispute and gives them the feeling that their sovereignty in foreign trade matters is not fundamentally affected. In reality, obstruction is difficult, and an isolated position in the midst of all the other CPs can rarely be sustained for a prolonged time.[56] The secrecy throughout the different stages of the DS procedures favours a climate of compromise and finally agreed solutions.

Shortcomings

One of the many flaws of the system is linked to this prevailing element of negotiation and consensus. Thus power-oriented and delaying tactics, which favour the country having taken measures inconsistent with GATT, have come up.[57] Linked counter attacks have become more common, whereas the number of final and binding decisions has decreased. Existing time limits are less often observed. Less rule-oriented settlements are often achieved outside agreements revealing a deliberate departure from the GATT rule of non-discrimination. The GATT DS procedures seem only to be successful in cases of minor importance.

In this rather unfavourable political climate the quality of some panel reports seems to have gotten worse, especially as the GATT system has become more defective by waivers, agreed departures from the rules, and special regimes. In this situation it is thought that experienced diplomats on the panels, who tend to understand their role more as conciliators than as interpretors of rules, do not provide the necessary confidence in an impartial DS procedure. In short, it seems necessary that a new consensus as to the substance of GATT law must be achieved during the forthcoming negotiations. The existing DS procedures cannot be a valid substitute for such a renewed consensus. For the time being it seems unlikely that the GATT DS procedures can generate a reliable and law-creating case law. In addition, DS procedures must be strengthened and improved if they are to regain the confidence of the CPs in an impartial, fair and speedy settlement of disputes. This, at the same time, is a necessary condition for the reliability of GATT rules for individual operators in the markets.

In summary, the merits and shortcomings of the GATT DS system are linked to the preponderance of negotiations and consensus which characterize the GATT system.[58] Within the various stages of the staggered central procedure under Article XXIII GATT only the middle stage, the panel procedure, has some impartial and judicial elements. But even this stage traditionally helps the parties to reach final settlements by negotiations. As has been seen above, the CJEC and other courts consider these procedures to be too flexible to justify a direct applicability of GATT rules and in favour of individual operators.

According to the Ministerial Declaration of 1986, the strengthening of the DS process is on the agenda of the New Round. But where to go? Are there any comparable models in other international organizations or multilateral treaties which could guide the ongoing negotiations?

COMPARATIVE ANALYSIS

What Is Comparable to GATT?

A recent collection of dispute settlement procedures in public international law mentions more than 100 agreed upon procedures between states and/or international organizations which, for the sake of the final settlement of disputes, have at least a quasi-judicial character.[59] The central GATT procedure under Article XXII et seq. is included. On the one hand, none of the other existing and drafted procedures is comparable to that of GATT in respect to structure and specific aims. On the other hand, GATT has no element in its DS procedures which, taken by itself, does not appear in at least one of the many other different procedures in one way or the other.

In order to have a valid comparison one would have to look at a worldwide interstate DS system which is related to international economic relations. There is none. Among international systems with specific economic aims one would have to exclude those operating only on a regional basis, which include the developed European systems. One would also have to disregard systems which operate on a worldwide basis, but within the framework of independent institutions of a given international organization such as the ILO, the World Bank, or the IMF. Procedures giving access to individuals, such as some of the above mentioned regional systems, or for example the International Center for the Settlement of Investment Disputes (ICSID), or some of the procedures under the Law of the Sea Convention are not comparable either. In short, GATT is unique.

Therefore, a comparative analysis can only point out different elements that have been positive in other institutionalized DS procedures. Such procedures could be procedures of (2) consultation and negotiation, (3) good offices and mediation, (4) inquiry, (5) conciliation, (6) arbitration and finally of (7) adjudication by permanent tribunals as specified in Article 33 of the Charter of the United Nations.

Consultations and Negotiations

Article XXII GATT urges the contracting parties under dispute to accord "sympathetic" consideration to any representation and to afford adequate opportunity of consultation. This first step in any DS procedure may even be considered to be an unwritten general obligation when parties under dispute are both contracting parties of the same treaty or organization.[60] Consultations and negotiations may still be necessary in order to find out whether a given difference becomes sufficiently specific to be called a dispute.[61] Diplomatic negotiations or consultations aiming at the settlement of disputes are by their very nature an informal art, that is to say, hardly any rules or patterns exist to which a comparative analysis could refer.[62]

Under GATT half of the disputes, that is about 100, which have been formally brought under the procedures have been settled by negotiation.[63] This success is due to the advantages which negotiations offer to the parties in dispute: They can control the process and outcome of the procedure, the result will have a maximum of acceptability and stability and will not be in the way for any ongoing long-term cooperative relations.[64]

Good Offices and Mediation

If the parties cannot resolve their dispute by negotiations they may seek the good offices of or mediation by a third party. Good offices may be offered by providing only additional channels of communication.

If the third party helps to clarify the matter and transmits its own suggestions and proposals to the parties in dispute, informal mediation may come close to the procedures of inquiry and conciliation.[65]

Under general international law mediation by a third party has been most successful in settling even highly political disputes in which just negotiations were not further possible, for example in the controversies of the Beagle-Channel, the Falklands/Malvinas, and the United States/ Iran hostages.

Under the GATT system the Understanding of 1979 (para. 8) urges the General Director to provide his good offices in every case in which a developing country is bringing a complaint against a developed country. In fact, the role of the CPs under Article XXIII is one of mediation although the contracting parties under dispute are participating in the deliberations on an equal footing. It will have to be examined whether the General Director or the GATT Secretariat or its Legal Service could be more involved in providing good offices and mediation to parties in dispute. In international organizations such a function very often is entrusted to the relevant institutions. Thus under Article 170 EEC Treaty any Member State which intends to bring an action against another Member State for an alleged infringement of the treaty first has to bring the matter before the EEC Commission. It is then the role of the Commission to consult with both states and to deliver a reasoned opinion.

Commissions of Inquiry

A more formal interference by a third party is provided for by the technique of inquiry. In abstract form, this procedure is particularly capable to establish facts which are in the core of a dispute. Inquiries were first formulated by the Hague Conventions of 1899 and 1907 as a procedure for the settlement of narrowly defined disputes, but in practice, states have adopted the technique of inquiry to provide a large range of solutions on legal issues as well as on facts. As flexible as this method appears to be, it has not been widely used in international DS practice.[66]

For an interesting example one may look at Article 26 of the ILO Constitution which, in the framework of the general ILO complaint procedure, provides for an inquiry. The Governing Body can appoint an independent Commission of Inquiry in order to find out whether in a given state the obligations under one of the ILO Conventions have not been complied with. The most recent and prominent example is the Commission of Inquiry which in 1985 was asked to find out whether in the Federal Republic of Germany access to the civil service is dependent

on the political conviction of a candidate. In the end of May 1987 the
Governing Body of the ILO has taken note of the inquiry report, which
gave detailed recommendations as to the modification of the German
pracrices. In this case, not only questions of fact had to be analyzed,
but also questions of law as to the compatibility of the German practices
with the ILO Convention No. 111. Thus, this inquiry has been similar
to the procedure of conciliation.

It might be worthwhile to analyze in which of the GATT DS procedures
merely issues of fact had been involved. Since disputes on the question
whether a market is disrupted or a market share has been diminished
arise regularly, an inquiry could be useful in helping the parties to
resolve the remaining legal aspects of their dispute. At present, Article
XXIII (2) urges the CPs "to investigate any matter under dispute." Under
this wording the CPs also could institute an independent Commission
of Inquiry that would be charged with clarifying the relevant facts. In
view of the large range of possible disputes under the system of GATT,
it does not seem appropriate to establish a permanent Commission of
Inquiry. The present practice of establishing panels ad hoc does give
the CPs, when determining the terms of reference, all the possibilities
which offer the technique of inquiry.[67]

Conciliation

The GATT panel procedures may be best compared to procedures of
conciliation that have been common under public international law since
the end of the first World War. These procedures do not have a great
record. Although such procedures are provided for in some 200 bilateral
treaties and in various multilateral treaties such as the Convention on
the Law of Treaties or on the Law of the Sea,[68] they have been applied
only in some twenty cases.

Parties may set up a commission or address themselves to an individual
person in order to proceed to an impartial examination of the dispute
and to attempt to define the terms of a settlement that could be acceptable
to both parties. The outcome of the procedure of conciliation is only a
proposal without binding effect. As to the terms of reference there are
significant differences that may either bring a conciliation close to
arbitration ("consultative arbitration") or only close to a form of an
institutionalized negotiation. Thus, there is a large number of procedures
from which elements for the reform of the GATT panel procedures can
be taken especially with the purpose of having a disinterested third
party involved. Practical experiences, however, are rare.

Judicial Settlement by Arbitration

Contrary to the foregoing techniques adjudication, by definition, leads to a binding decision by either an ad hoc arbitral tribunal or by a permanent court. Thus the outcome is not dependent on the will of the parties; they may only participate in the procedures. In the end the tribunal decides the case. Adjudication in both forms has a number of advantages and disadvantages which cannot be dealt with in this context.[69]

Within the procedure of arbitration the parties themselves set up the machinery to handle their dispute. The parties may influence the selection of the arbitrators, the terms of reference, and the procedure to be followed. The parties may agree, as in the case of the BENELUX treaty, to take arbitrators only from a standing roster.[70] They may agree to select arbitrators who suit both sides or to have at least one of the arbitrators nominated by each side. In regard to GATT various models exist for the structuring of the panel procedure. Even a panel determination will be considered to be final and binding—if the parties to the dispute would agree prior to the examination of the case or subsequently.[71] However, contracting parties do not seem to be prepared to have a panel decide their dispute. The main task of the panels still will be to propose a solution acceptable to both sides and, in the end, to the CPs. The "Chicken War Case" is the only case in which it seemed that the disputing parties agreed to have the panel decide their dispute by a binding advisory opinion.[72]

Judicial Settlement by Permanent Tribunals

Judicial settlement by a permanent tribunal also leads to a binding decision. The jurisdiction may be compulsory on the basis of a treaty or voluntary on the basis of an ad hoc consent of the parties. A permanent tribunal is readily available. It offers a large degree of independence and due to its permanent composition it is able to develop a consistent case law. Undoubtedly, adjudication by permanent courts favours the enforcement of rules of international law. In addition, by simply being available, such binding arrangements will help to avoid disputes and induce the parties to settle these by other forms of consensual procedures.[73]

In recent times state practice seems more willing to accept this binding DS procedure, but states are still reluctant to bring cases before the relevant courts. The signing of the Law of the Sea Convention was a remarkable step in this direction. Although this Convention relates to economic matters and is supposed to be operated on a worldwide basis, it is, however, no precedent for GATT. In the Law of the Sea Convention states are going to accept binding judicial settlements by standing tribunals especially under two circumstances:

1. The first relates to the protection of one's nationals operating outside the own territory, e.g. in waters under foreign jurisdiction where otherwise it would be difficult to assure legal protection in their favour. An express exception for the jurisdiction of the relevant tribunal is made in regard to the exercise of sovereign rights or jurisdiction of the coastal state.[74]
2. The second area relates to legal protection against the acts of the International Seabed Authority (ISA) to which certain powers will have to be transferred. These acts may even be attacked by individual operators.[75]

Both situations are different from those which present themselves under GATT procedures: In GATT the exercise of a state's sovereign economic policy is in dispute, which may fall under the exception in regard to the Law of the Sea Convention. There are no powers transferred to GATT as is the case of the ISA, therefore, there is no access of individuals. Apart from these fundamental differences, the Law of the Sea Convention could be analysed in reference to detailed rules such as on interim measures and on other matters.[76] A detailed conciliation procedure is also provided for,[77] which concerns a nonobligatory stage prior to the judicial stages. This procedure can give a technical model for the GATT panel procedure since both end with a nonbinding report containing conclusions of fact and law as well as with recommendations to the parties in dispute.

In regard to the *International Court of Justice (ICJ)* and its suitability to decide cases under GATT law, reference has been made to advisory opinions and to the possibility of submitting cases to a special chamber of the Court in accordance with Article 26 of the Statute.[78] The procedure before a special chamber is rather flexible. The judges, all from the ICJ, would also be able to base their judgment on equitable considerations, if the applicable (GATT) law would allow.[79] The chamber procedure has to end with the binding judgment, which so far would not be acceptable to most of the contracting parties to GATT, and states would certainly like to have more influence on the determination of the judges as is available in the case of arbitration.

As to the *advisory opinion*, Article 96 of the UN Charter presupposes that GATT would have to be considered as a specialized agency under the UN system. This would certainly not be an insurmountable obstacle. However, in general it remains questionable whether the ICJ is an adequate institution for being involved in the GATT DS procedure as it has evolved since 1948. At that time a reference to the ICJ had been provided for in the Havanna Charter (1948),[80] but this reference had been omitted when drafting the GATT agreement. This decision reflects the overall practice of states which *never* have submitted cases relating to their general commercial or financial relations to the Permanent Court of International Justice (PCIJ) or to the ICJ.[81]

To conclude, even under a DS procedure by a permanent tribunal it is possible to add an additional stage of negotiations in order to reach a final consent between the parties. The judgment of the ICJ in the Continental Shelf of the North Sea Case of 1969 was followed by negotiations by the three parties involved on the basis of the binding legal guidelines given by the Court.[82]

The *Court of Justice of the European Communities (CJEC)* certainly has to decide on economic and foreign trade matters. The EC treaties have even been modelled according to the basis principles of GATT.[83] The EC Member States have learned to have such sensitive disputes settled by a binding court decision. The CJEC apparently found a satisfactory balance between the various interests, especially by leaving a rather large economic discretion either to the EC's institutions or to the Member States when measures under national law had to be controlled.[84] Of course, this judicial process is anchored firmly in the regional process of integration between homogeneous Member States and, consequently, this can be no model for GATT. It may be discussed, however, whether the specific support the judges of CJEC get by the participation of the EC Commission and eventually the Council in the procedures may be considered in regard to the panel procedure.[85] In addition, the Advocate General supports the Court by his extensive conclusions. It is thus not surprising that the CJEC judgments are strongly influenced by considerations which are pro integratione. Could such an influence in favour of an objective interpretation of the GATT rules be recommended for the panel procedures, whether by the participation of the Secretariat or another independent institution?

Other elements are equally worth considering in regard to GATT, such as the strict time limits existing for the parties (which in some quarters are considered to be too short and strict),[86] or for the surveillance procedure under Article 169 of the EEC Treaty. Another element is the effective operation of procedures on interim measures.[87] The *access given to individuals* and, more in detail, the various conditions set up for individual complaints to be admissable may be considered in regard to some of the GATT procedures.[88]

This same access exists in the case of the *European Court of Human Rights (ECHR)*. Any individual's case is considered by the European Commission of Human Rights first, a filter which was passed by only

1 percent out of the 11,819 complaints by the close of 1985. Even this 1 percent of the cases allowed the Court to develop an impressive case law on the interpretation of the European Convention on Human Rights.

It does not seem appropriate to refer further to other regional models. None of them in the abstract would suit GATT, since GATT does not have any rule-making or rule-interpreting institution which may act with binding authority or which could develop a case law with gap-filling functions. Only some procedural elements are worth being considered with respect to a reform of the GATT DS procedures.

Functions of a Comparative Analysis

GATT, as has been demonstrated, is unique with respect to other worldwide organizations operating in the field of economic relations. Its DS procedures contain various elements of consultation, negotiation, good offices, mediation and conciliation. Only this mixture of various procedures has made it possible for the DS procedures to provide for a satisfactory rule-oriented settlement as well as for results which have helped to restore the balance of benefits and legitimate expectations under GATT. In view of the shortcomings of the GATT system, the various DS procedures agreed upon under general international law may serve as a source of reference and offer at least elements of reform of the neuralgic points of the existing procedures. These will be listed in the following section and discussed in the light of comparable experiences.

PROPOSALS FOR STRENGTHENING THE GATT DS PROCEDURES

The Ministerial Declaration calls for improving and strengthening the existing rules and procedures. The first issue will be to examine whether the various aims of the DS procedures will have to be maintained or altered. Although the need for more reliable and enforceable rules will become evident, it seems that a purely judicial DS procedure would be unacceptable under the present political and economic circumstances.[89] Thus rule compliance will remain *only one* of the aims of the DS procedure. The mutually accepted settlement will remain an equally important goal. Apart from this underlying understanding a number of improvements seem possible.

The Differentiation of Procedures

The proliferation of procedures under the various GATT agreements has been regretted.[90] More authoritative, predictable, and less confusing decisions could be expected from a uniform central procedure covering the whole field of GATT activities.

However, one cannot be sure whether such a centralization may be beneficial and necessary. Certainly not all the rules under the existing GATT lend themselves to an adjudicatory system.[91] On the contrary, contracting parties could try to experiment with improved rules of DS in sectors of minor importance, for example, they could accept panel reports as binding. This would come close to arbitration.[92] Such a sector of minor importance could be the field of technical non-tariff barriers which may affect in principle individuals and small groups, but normally would not raise important issues of national trade policy.[93]

Even the number of contracting parties participating in the DS procedures could vary. For example a limited number of them could agree to adhere to stricter rules in their reciprocal relationship. Positive experiments could influence other contracting parties to expand various forms of DS to the entire GATT DS system. Of course, any experiment in specific sectors would require that the different procedures would not be linked to cases under review in other procedures. Finally it may be foreseen that any procedure could end up before the CPs for the sake of the cohesiveness of the GATT DS system.[94]

Interim Measures

In contrast to other DS procedures, no specific provisions on interim measures exist under GATT.[95] Consequently, parties may be tempted to use delaying tactics or may be forced to agree to "voluntary" agreements. The present Understanding of 1979 (para. 20) calls upon the panels, in case of urgency, to deliver their findings within a period of normally three months, which is already a very short time limit when compared to other DS procedures in international economic law.[96] It may be considered whether, in the case of an urgent complaint, a party should have the right to appeal to the CPs directly for an interim decision such as granting a cooling-off-period. Even provisional retaliating measures may be granted to a complaining party, particularly when the defending party delays the DS procedures without justification.

Stages of Mediation or Conciliation

In regard to an interstate dispute, Article 170 of the EEC Treaty provides that before going to the Court the parties have to address the EC Commission, which has to mediate and to give an opinion to the parties. A similar function could be entrusted to the Director General of the GATT Secretariat or to any other institution or person before a case is dealt with in the formal DS procedure, that is in the more stringent panel procedure as referred to in the following part. Thus the panel procedure could be kept free of efforts to find political solutions to disputes.

Panel Procedure

It is likely that contracting parties will not change substantially the various stages of the DS procedure. The panel procedure, however, can be improved in order to give more weight to its quasi-judicial findings. Although even in the future the reports will not have binding force, it is certainly possible to make them more credible. The more judicial this intermediate stage can be, the more the outcome will be able to influence the final stage before the CPs. Various improvements are examined below.

a) A *"right to a panel,"* already a major topic of the Tokyo negotiations, has not yet been recognized in the general DS procedure under Article XXIII GATT. However, the standing practice has been to refer such a matter to a panel if so requested by a complaining party directly concerned.[97] Such a right could even be given to an Attorney General or a contracting party in the interest of depersonalizing the dispute and to bring before GATT any bilateral agreement contrary to the GATT rules (VERs a.o.).[98]

b) As to the *composition of panels*, it has been sensible to choose panelists who do not have the nationality of one of the disputing parties or who have not been chosen by either of the parties concerned.[99] Above all, governmental representatives should not be chosen as panelists in order to guarantee a complete neutrality of the panel.[100] The establishment of standing panels would encourage the quasi-judicial function and probably also improve the quality of the panel reports. The latter is a necessary condition for the establishment of any meaningful case-law. The existing roster of nongovernmental panelists could be considered to be exclusive. There is no need for ad hoc panelists to be added to the panel by the disputing parties. The parties concerned will have sufficient opportunity to express their opinions during the final deliberations of the CPs. Strict time limits and mechanisms should be agreed upon in order to ensure that the composition of the panel will not be obstructed by the parties concerned.

c) In regard to the specific *panel procedures*, various improvements should be considered.

First, with respect to the *intervention of third-party states,* it should be clarified whether they should have a right to intervene and under which conditions a panel could refuse their demand for intervention.

Second, *time limits* should be agreed upon for the determination of the terms of reference, which could be, unless in exceptional cases, a standard set of terms, and for the written and oral observations of the parties involved. Yet for the overall length of the panel procedure it has been impossible so far to fix any precise time limits.[101] It may be possible to set such time limits in areas which deal with rather technical matters normally not involving much fact-finding or political considerations. In general the CPs will only be able to give indications and leave it to the sense of responsibility of the panelists to conclude the procedure as quickly as possible. No comparable time limits seem to exist in regard to any other DS procedures under public international law.

Third, a *standard set of procedural rules* would contribute to the shortening and the granting of more uniformity of the panel procedures. Thus, one could try to codify the various texts relating to the DS procedures and then try to reach agreement on substantial improvements. Such a code may even be established outside the ongoing negotiations during the New Round. In referring to such an informal text panels could develop a standing practice. Typical items would be, for example, rules on the burden of proof, on the secrecy of the procedure, on the admissibility of dissenting opinions, on costs, and on others.[102]

Fourth, regarding the *investigating powers of panels* the Understanding of 1979 (para. 16) has clarified the matter by asking the panels to make an objective assessment of the case before them. Since all contracting parties of GATT are interested in the outcome of any panel procedure, it would not be adequate to have the panels limited to a purely contradictory procedure. It remains to be seen whether there are still improvements possible with respect to the investigating powers of disclosure and verification of the underlying facts.

Finally, the GATT Secretariat, acting as *amicus curiae* of the panels, should contribute to a larger extent to the clarification of facts and underlying law.[103] A more specific role could be assigned to the Director General or to the Legal Advisor. Comparative analysis has revealed a number of different ways in which a judicial institution may be supported by a neutral representative of the respective common interests.

d) As to the *final report of the panel,* its persuasive force depends largely on their legal quality.[104] The panel should be restricted to decide only under legal terms in order to introduce into the whole DS procedure on reliable rule-oriented element. Yet, it has always been the practice of panels to continue to look for amicable settlements at any stage and to consult regularly with the parties. Thus panels have offered their assistance to any consent settlement before finalizing the panel report.

However, in view of the establishment of a more reliable case law it would be advisable, if not necessary, to *keep the legal functions of the panels separate from* the ongoing effort to reach *amicable solutions.*[105] The ambiguous terms of reference, as they are laid down in the Understanding of 1979 (para. 10), should therefore include a clearer reference to define a solution under the law of GATT. Although panel decisions have not and possibly will not have binding force, they may well serve as a source of reference. Their value as such a source will depend entirely on their legal quality and consistency.

Another question will be whether panels should try to base a decision on considerations of equity if a settlement under legal terms appears to be unsatisfactory.[106]

If a complaining party withdraws its case, it might be considered whether the panel should finalize its report in order to give legal guidance to future cases. A comparative analysis would show, however, that international tribunals have to recognize the right of states to withdraw a claim at any stage of the procedure. The sole exception to this is the European and American Human Rights Courts which, according to their rules, may formally decide and possibly refuse the admissibility of a unilateral or even a joint *declaration of discontinuance.* Instead these Courts may continue the proceedings in the interest of further clarifying human rights standards. Yet, even in regard to these procedures, there is considerable dispute. Arguably, these Courts may not continue interstate disputes if an amicable solution would have been found.[107]

In the case of GATT, the question of the admissibility of a declaration of discontinuance may only arise if under a future regime private complaints will be acceptable. Under the present system, and in the forseeable future, procedures may be terminated at any stage.[108]

The Decisions of the CPs

The third and final stage of the GATT DS procedure lies in the hands of the CPs. Under Article XXIII (2) the CPs may give recommendations or appropriate rulings on the basis of the panel reports, which, in effect, only have the legal value of *advisory opinions,*[109] unless the parties to the dispute agreed in advance to accept the findings of the panel as binding.

In view of the janus-faced character of the procedures, the CPs may deviate from the findings of the panels. The CPs are not adapted to play the role of an objective guardian of GATT law, because their deliberations are based equally on policy and equity considerations and not on purely legal grounds. The CPs will continue to find the best solution which often is not the legal one since this might well appear to be devisive. Consensus still seems to guarantee an adequate solution that has the highest degree of acceptability and stability for the parties in dispute and that will influence favourably their bilateral long-term trade relations. Consensus reflects the collective responsibility of the CPs for the functioning of the GATT system.

Nonetheless, this advantage will have to be balanced against the danger of a normative digression and a loss of credibility of the system if the CPs agree on solutions not in conformity with GATT rules on which the individual operators might have relied. And in addition, only an adjudicatory decision would undisputedly bind the national courts. It remains to be seen to what extent decisions of the CPs, possibly being qualified as supplementing agreements under GATT, would be able to bind a national judiciary.[110] As a first step it should be agreed that panel decisions will become binding if the CPs do not take any other decision within a certain time limit.

In 1982 the United States backed a proposal under which parties to a dispute must abstain in the final vote of the CPs.[111] Major improvements of the whole procedure are difficult to imagine as long as the loser in the proceedings has the possibility of blocking the final outcome. The resulting risk to any abstaining party would certainly not be very great due to the interdependence of all the parties. Even an isolated veto, which has not much solid ground, could not be upheld for a prolonged time, this at least is the practical experience in the EC Council.

The possibility of opening an appeal against decisions of the CPs, as is the case in other international organizations like ICAO and ICSID,[112] will not be an item of discussion. Instead, the CPs may propose another panel with other experts to review the case or to give an opinion on still unsettled issues.

The Exclusiveness of GATT DS Procedures

A delicate issue is the problem of whether GATT DS procedures should be exclusive. Under GATT there is no specific rule. In the New Round the negotiating parties could agree that any specific procedure under a special agreement in conformity with GATT would exclude any parallel access to the general procedure under Article XXIII GATT. It is an open question, however, whether any procedure under the GATT system should be considered as being exclusive in regard to other DS procedures under general public international law. A critical question is the admissability of measures of coercion, if in the view of one of the parties the GATT procedure has produced an "unsatisfactory" or no result at all.

Article 219 of the EEC Treaty contains a specific rule on exclusiveness. Article 26 of the ICSID Convention also provides for the general principle that arbitration under ICSID is the *sole* means of settling a dispute. Divergent opinions exist only in regard to the exclusiveness of interim measures being recommended by the arbitral tribunal.[113] There are good reasons for a clear rule that would confirm the exclusiveness of the GATT procedures thereby eliminating any recourse to general means under public international law. But shall this exclusion apply only for the time of an ongoing procedure, or shall it even apply after a case has been closed or unduly delayed?[114]

There are good reasons to leave this question open. Although one may be in favour of the exclusiveness of GATT procedures, such an approach would be unrealistic if the GATT procedure did not come to an end in a reasonable time. In regard to the special procedures under the GATT codes, any rule of exclusiveness should not limit the recourse of the parties to the central procedure under Article XXII/XXIII GATT.[115]

Under comparative terms similar disputes exist whether or not specific procedures shall be regarded as exclusive and final, particularly in the field of human rights procedures.[116]

Sanctions

In regard to sanctions other than those provided for in Article XXIII (2) GATT, there is no reason to change the present situation. It has been stressed, and with good reason, that sanctions and resultant counter-sanctions may lead to an additional blow to free trade, the remedy being in the end more harmful than the disease.[117] And above all, sanctions often damage those who are not responsible for the dispute in question. Any change of the status quo would probably dissuade governments from availing themselves of the DS process under GATT.[118] Another question concerns the need for better surveillance of the performance of states in accordance with the decisions of the CPs.[119] As it has been observed GATT never will be the primary enforcer of its rules.[120] GATT is based on the consensual adherence of the contracting parties to the agreed rules which are designed to guide their respective national trade policies.

Developing Countries

The particularly difficult situation of developing countries in respect to the complicated DS procedures will again be on the agenda of the

New Round. This question is closely related to the above mentioned role of the GATT Secretariat.

Access of Individuals

Access of individuals is a final topic for improving the existing procedures.[121] The success of the ICSID Convention which grants access of individuals to a procedure of arbitration with foreign states may be encouraging. Between 1972–1987 twenty-four cases have been settled; ten cases are still pending.[122] Although in principle one may be in favour of trying to find an adequate access for individuals, it will be extremely difficult to reach an agreement on this question, and only a cautious, step-by-step approach seems possible. One could consider an individual's right to complain either to a national authority against national measures violating GATT rules or an individual's right to compel the national government to take actions against a foreign government which may be in breach of GATT law. Reference has been made to Article X (3b) GATT which obliges each contracting party to maintain internal judicial procedures as to custom matters.[123] This approach should be enlarged to other areas.

Access of individual should also be discussed in regard to the GATT DS procedures, of course only after the exhaustion of local remedies.[124] Even under the law as it stands panels have the right to ask for information from any private person.[125] Since state complaints often are a form of hidden diplomatic protection, it seems that panels could find a way also under the given procedures and under their powers of investigation to hear any individual directly concerned on a more systematical basis.[126] Particularly a preliminary procedure, which could link national courts to the GATT procedures, should be considered when national courts would directly apply GATT law.

Petitions by individuals or national industries have not, so far, been a subject of discussion. In regard to specific codes, as for example the NTB Code, individuals could have the possibility to ask for an authentic interpretation of the agreed rules. Yet, it appears that national governments would like to act as a filter for any such approach. Thus, preliminary procedures which may be open to national courts seem more appropriate.

A more intense involvement of individuals under national and GATT procedures would emphasize the constitutional function of GATT law and lead to increased case law providing more reliability for the individual's economic decisions. Access for individuals, however, should not lead to arbitrary political pressures or to political privileges for groups that are more effectively organized than others.

Evolutionary Improvements of DS Procedures

In summing up, most of the aforementioned proposals and suggestions for a strengthening of GATT DS procedures could be considered by practitioners and diplomats as not very promising. These proposals are meant to offer models and to provide stimulation on the basis of an immense comparative stock as it exists in present international economic relations. The contracting parties will only consent to a gradual improvement and evolutionary approach to strengthening the disciplines under the DS procedures. Any DS procedure with binding authority independent of the will of the parties might still appear to many contracting states as being too risky to their trade policies. Although it does seem that the interdependence between nations in the field of international trade is growing, faster than might be expected, one should not ask too much too soon. The more nations are forced to cooperate, the more their mutual legal obligations should be enforceable within a reliable legal framework. Particularly in cases of minor importance on which the contracting parties have concluded a detailed and closely-knit agreement it could be in the common interest of all to have a DS procedure that is readily available and efficient in the independent handling and deciding of such disputes. One essential condition for the efficiency of the process is, however, that the capacity of the system, and especially of the GATT secretariat, is adapted to the number of DS proceedings.

The search for a more effective framework for the settlement of disputes does not necessarily mean that legal experts or judges become responsible for the overall trade policy. A DS procedure which could be dominated by the element of negotiations often can lead to unfair and one-sided settlements. For the time being the present panel procedure under GATT, which has to consider from time to time important issues of worldwide trade relations, has proved to be an imaginative base on which one may rely in the future. The more professional the legal stage within the panel procedure can become, the more it will have persuasive authority to influence and convince the CPs to follow the agreed rules.

The future choice is not between an evolving legalistic system, on the one side, and a diplomatically steered system of negotiation and consensus, on the other side. If the contracting parties stick to the basic understanding that GATT law is law, there may be no future for the trading system without elements of transparent and effective legal DS procedures. The evolutionary trend toward more effective international institutions is irreversible. Bilateralism again is no solution.

CONCLUSION

An interdisciplinary view, as is this volume's approach, will help to clarify the relationship between law and economy. This relationship is one of permanent tension. Would more efficient or even more judicial DS procedures have guaranteed fewer economic disputes? Would stricter DS rules be more helpful in avoiding disputes or would stricter rules pressure the parties to settle their disputes by prior negotiations? Would better economic rules have avoided many of the unfortunate disputes under the present system of GATT? The comparative analysis has pointed out a great number of systems each of which has developed different techniques to guarantee respect for the rule of law without suffocating the legitimate breath of the economy.

International trade relations are increasingly inseparably linked to national economies. States are giving up more and more of their freedom to act as they want. Any bilateral trade relationship has repercussions for other trade relationships. The development of the world market, influenced by a multitude of uncontrollable actors, causes a loss of sovereignty.[127] If states want to avoid this situation, they must try to influence the trade policies of other states through commonly agreed upon rules. Consequently, states then must try to enforce these rules through adequate DS procedures. Thus the creeping loss of sovereignty may be compensated to some extent, but only if the agreed rules are observed by all sides.

Additionally this dependence on foreign trade relations will have, at the same time, repercussions on the *internal constitutional order*. States will be increasingly constrained to remain open and to adopt institutions conducive to efficient competition on world markets.[128] These constraints will be felt even by states which traditionally maintain a state trading system. Therefore, it is not surprising that in these countries the idea of a more stringent international DS settlement, even by judicial procedures, seems to become acceptable.

The constitutional entrenchment of the international trade rules can also contribute to a liberal internal economic order, if during the forthcoming Round the rules negotiated are clear enough to be applicable in judicial proceedings.[129] Under this condition even the absence of any sanctions would not hinder the effective realization of the common aims. If the ongoing negotiations, however, would turn only to "strengthening the DS procedures as a substitute for failed negotiations on substantive rules"[130]—a result which would not have to be paid by trade concessions!—then the negotiations as a whole will have failed.

Is it time to propose a World Trade Charter including a strict DS procedure? Realists would hesitate. From the experience gained from helping the European Parliament drafting a rather utopian proposal for a Treaty on the European Union (1984), one may be of an opposite opinion: A far-reaching proposal at a well-chosen moment has chances to accomplish a measure of moderate progress. Such progress has been achieved by the adoption of the Single European Act (1987). This Act was drafted primarily in reaction to the project of the European Parliament.[131] For the Uruguay Round, however, a World Trade Charter would come too late, but there will be further rounds.

Notes

1. R.E. HUDEC, "Transcending the Ostensible," Some Reflections on the Nature of Litigation Between Governments, The Melvin C. Steen Professorship of Law, Inaugural Lecture, April 9, 1987, in Minnesota Law Review, no. 226 (1987), p. 226.

2. See J.H. JACKSON, in E.-U. PETERSMANN/M. HILF (eds.) The New GATT Round on Multilateral Trade Negotiations, Economic and Legal Aspects, Kluwer (1988).

3. Cf. HUDEC, supra n. 1, 2, discussing the raising level of resistance and dissatisfaction with the panel procedures under GATT.

4. R.E. HUDEC, Legal Issues in U.S./EC Trade Policy: GATT Litigation 1960–1985, in R.E. BALDWIN et al. (eds.). Issues in U.S.-EC Trade Relations, University of Chicago Press for the National Bureau of Economic Research (1989); idem, supra n. 1, 19 et seq. noting that the Subsidies Code was prepared over disagreements that could not be resolved and that, therefore, unsatisfactory DS procedures were to be expected; M. COCCIA, Settlement of Disputes in GATT under the Subsidies Code: Two Panel Reports on EEC Export Subsidies, Georgia Journal of International and Comparative Law 16 (1986) 1 et seq. It has to be noted that most of the "long-standing" unsettled disputes have been finally resolved (see the reference to the cases EC Preferences for Mediterranean Citrus Products, the U.S. Manufactoring Clause and the Pasta Case by J.H. JACKSON/W.J. DAVEY, Supplementary Memorandum (August 1987) to the Casebook on Legal Problems of International Economic Relations, 2nd ed. (St. Paul, Minn. 1986) 4 et seq.

5. J.H. JACKSON, World Trade and the Law of GATT (Indianapolis, Ind. 1969) 163 et seq; idem, Governmental Disputes in International Trade Relations: A Proposal in the Context of GATT, Journal of World Trade Law 13 (1979) 1 et seq.; E. McGOVERN, Dispute Settlement in the Adjudication or Negotiation, in: M. HILF/F.G. JACOBS/E.-U. PETERSMANN, The European Community and GATT (Deventer 1986) 73 et seq.; G. BARCERO, Trade Laws, GATT and the Management of Trade Disputes Between the U.S. and EEC, Yearbook of European Law 5 (1985) 149 et seq.; and R.E. HUDEC, GATT Dispute Settlement After the Tokyo Round: An Unfinished Business, Cornell International Law

Journal 13 (1980), 145 et seq. The most recent contribution analyzing the existing procedures and possible reforms is E.-U. PETERSMANN, Experience and Proposals on GATT Dispute Settlement Procedures, in: H. CORBET/G. DELA DEHES (eds.), The European Community and the Uruguay Negotiations (1988).

6. Compare Basic Instruments and Selected Documents (BISD) 14S/18 (1966) regarding a special regime for disputes in which the plaintiff is a developing country; (BISD) 26S/210 (1980) with the Understanding Regarding Notification, Consultation, Dispute Settlement and Surveillance with annex on Agreed Description of the Customary Practice of the GATT in the Field of Dispute Settlement (loc. cit. 215 et seq.); BISD 29 S/13 (1982) concerning the Ministerial Declaration of 29.11.1982 and BISD 31 S/9 et seq. (1984) concerning the decision of the Contracting Parties of 30.11.1984 on Dispute Settlement procedures. For an overall view cf. the Analytical Index, Notes on the Drafting, Interpretation, Application of the Articles of the General Agreement, published by the Contracting Parties to GATT (GATT/LEG/2, Geneva 1985).

7. GATT, Newsletter FOCUS, 41 (1986) 4; BISD 33S/19.

8. See supra p. 6: Doubts as to the quality of GATT law arise in regard to the many agreed departures, bilateral or sectoral arrangements being inconsistent with GATT rules; for an overall balance cf. O. LONG, Law and its Limitations in the GATT Multilateral Trade System (Dordrecht 1985). On the regimes "à la carte" which the Contracting Parties prevail themselves under the proliferation of the special regimes under GATT see T. FLORY, L'évolution des régimes juridiques du GATT, Journal du droit international 113 (1986) 340 et seq.

9. This is at least true for the German Federal Constitutional Court deciding cases in the field of diplomatic protection (see BVerfGE 55, 349 Hess-Case), and for the Court of Justice of the European Communities, e.g., Case 48/84 Federal Republic of Germany/Commission, Judgment of 14.10.1987, in the field of state aids. For the general trend see R. WIETHOLTER, Materialization and Proceduralization in Modern Law, in G. Teubner (ed.), Dilemmas of Law in the Welfare State (Berlin/New York 1986) 221 et seq. and R. DOLZER, Verfassungskonkretisierung durch das Bundesverfassungsgericht und durch politische Verfassungsorgane (Heidelberg 1982).

10. C. BAUDENBACHER, Verfahren als Alternative zur Verrechtlichung im Wirtschaftsrecht?, Zeitschrift für Rechtspolitik 19 (1986) 301 et seq., determining "consent-settlement" as a typical instrument for settling disputes within a welfare state.

11. See R.B. BILDER, Some Limitations of Adjudication as an International Dispute Settlement Technique, Virginia Journal of International Law 23 (1982/83) 1, 10, referring especially to parties involved in long-term continuing relationships which, in effect, is the typical relationship between states under international economic law.

12. International Legal Materials 21 (1982) 1261 et seq.; see especially R. BERNHARDT, Law of the Sea, Settlement of Disputes, in R. Bernhardt (ed.), Encyclopedia of Public International Law, Installment 1 (Amsterdam a.o. 1981) 133 et seq. with further references.

13. Only two interstate disputes based on Art. 170 EEC Treaty have been brought before the CJEC; in only one of these cases has there been a final

decision, see Case 141/78 France v. United Kingdom (1979) ECR 2923 et seq.: cf. 20th General Report on the Activities of the European Communities 1986 (Brussels 1987) 414. According to this report the total number of cases brought before the CJEC has been 5499.

14. Cf. I. v. MÜNCH, in I. v. Münch (ed.), Grundgesetz-Kommentar, vol. 1, 3rd ed. (Munich 1985) Art. 1, n. 43.

15. Cf. HUDEC, supra n. 5, 150 et seq.; JACKSON, supra n. 5. Governmental Disputes 3 et seq., and idem, the Crumbling Institutions of the Liberal Trade System, Journal of World Trade Law 12 (1978) 93, 98 et seq., supporting the evolutionary hypothesis from power to rule. A well-balanced view is given by LONG, supra n. 8, 64 et seq. reconciling pragmatism with legal construction. F. ROESSLER, L'attitude des États Unies et de la CEE devant le droit du GATT, in J. BOURRINET (ed.), Les relations Communauté européenne/États-Unies (1987) 43 et seq., reports that the EC and the United States have consistently taken different positions on the juridical character of the DS procedure under GATT. For a clear rule-oriented approach which limits the discretion of governments, see J.H. JACKSON's comments in Multilateral Trade Negotiations: Dispute Settlement, Proceedings of the 74th Annual Meeting of the American Society of International Law (1980) 136 et seq., 145.

16. The question of direct applicability of GATT law is complex and should be discussed from different angles, cf. M. HILF, The Application of GATT within the Member States of the European Community, with special reference to the Federal Republic of Germany, in M. Hilf/F.G. Jacobs/E.-U. Petersmann (eds.), The European Community and GATT (Deventer a.o. 1986) 153 et seq., 173 et seq., with further references; for G. de LACHARRIÈRE, Case for a Tribunal to Assist in Settling Trade Disputes. The World Economy 8 (1986) 339 et seq., 349, a direct application of GATT rules by national courts would not correspond to the more flexible application of GATT rules by the Contracting Parties.

17. Cf. ROESSLER, supra n. 15, 45 note 7 citing a member of the EC Commission who declared that one should not transform GATT into a tribunal; E.-U. PETERSMANN, The EEC as a GATT Member—Legal Conflicts Between GATT-Law and European Community Law, in M. Hilf/F.G. Jacobs/E.-U. Petersmann (eds.), The European Community and GATT (Deventer a.o. 1986) 43 et seq.

18. An interesting demonstration is given by U. EVERLING, Zur direkten innerstaatlichen Wirkung der EG-Richtlinien: Ein Beispiel richterlicher Rechtsfortbildung auf der Basis gemeinsamer Rechtsgrundsätze, in B. BÖRNER u.a. (Hrsg.), Festschrift für Karl Carstens (Köln 1984) et seq.

19. Arts. 113 et seq. EEC Treaty provide that the Council shall act by a qualified majority when acting in the field of the common commercial policy. Yet the Council is trying to reach unanimity if "very important interests of one or more partners are at stake" (so-called Luxembourg Accords of 1966).

20. Supra n. 15.

21. For references see HILF, supra n. 16, and M. MARESCEAU, The GATT in the Case-Law of the European Court of Justice, in M. Hilf/F.G. Jacobs/E.-U. Petersmann, The European Community and GATT (Deventer u.a. 1986), 107 et seq.

22. Cf. C.-D. EHLERMANN, Application of GATT-Rules in the European Community, loc. cit., 127 et seq.

23. Cases 21-24/72 International Fruit Company (1972) ECR 1219 1227 and Case 9/73 Schlüter (1973) ECR 35, 1156; doubts as to this concept of priority are expressed by J.H.J. BOURGEOIS, Effects of International Agreements in European Community Law: Are the Dice Cast? in Michigan Law Review Association (ed.), The Art of Governance, Festschrift zu Ehren von Eric Stein (Baden-Baden 1987) 113, 132 et seq.

24. See M. HILF, Europäische Gemeinschaften und internationale Streitbeilegung, in R. Bernhardt u.a. (eds.), Völkerrecht als Rechtsordnung, Internationale Gerichtsbarkeit, Menschenrechte, Festschrift für Hermann Mosler (Berlin u.a. 1983) 387, 425 et seq., arguing that negotiation and consultation come close to the traditional role of the Commission in negotiating international treaties, whereas all acts as in a procedure of arbitration would probably have to be taken by the EC Council since arbitration leads to a binding result which can normally only be achieved by the conclusion of a treaty which is in the Council's powers.

25. Section 301 as it stands under the Trade and Tariff Act of 1984 does not give the individual the right to force the executive to open a GATT DS procedure. It will have to be seen whether the proposed Trade Act of 1987 will limit the discretion of the executive to open DS procedures under GATT.

26. For a comparison of Section 301 with the New Trade Policy Instrument (Official Journal 1984, No. L 252/1) see M.C.E.J. BRONCKERS, Selective Safeguard Measures in Multilateral Trade Relations (Deventer u.a. 1985) 157 et seq., and M. HILF, International Trade Disputes and the Individual: Private Party Involvement in National and International Procedures Regarding Unfair Foreign Trade Practices, in H. Hauser (ed.), Protectionism and Structural Adjustment (Grüsch 1986) 279 et seq.

27. Referred to by JACKSON, supra n. 15, Crumbling Institutions 102.

28. Cf. ROESSLER, supra n. 15.

29. For references see HILF, supra n. 24, 402-412, giving examples of bilateral and multilateral treaties.

30. Loc. cit., 412-417. The EEC and Switzerland have agreed, in principle, to establish a tribunal to interpret a projected agreement over the Laying-Up Fund for the Navigation on the Rhine (Official Journal No. C 208/3 of 3.9.1976). The CJEC has ruled that this projected agreement is not in conformity with the EEC Treaty: see Advisory Opinion 1/76 of 26.4.1977 (1977) ECR 741, 762. The CJEC agreed with the idea of creating a specific court under the agreement, but it had reservations as to the particular structure of the court to be created.

31. The EEC signed the Law of the Sea Convention on Dec. 7, 1984: cr. W. Graf VITZTHUM. The European Economic Community, the Law of the Sea Development and the New International Economic Order, in T. Oppermann/E.-U. Petersmann (eds.), Reforming the International Economic Order (Berlin 1987), 243 et seq.

32. For a detailed analysis of the relevant practice see HUDEC, supra n. 4.

33. JACKSON, supra n. 15, Crumbling Institutions 101, still wondered whether the hesitation of the EEC to accept international constraints was, at the time, a reaction to the then delicate and unstable process of integration.

34. For a detailed comparison see BARCERO, supra n. 5, 148, 152.

35. See The GATT Negotiations and the U.S. Trade Policy, The Congress of the United States, Congressional Budget Office (Washington, D.C. 1987) and especially the report of the United States International Trade Commission, Review of the Effectiveness of Trade Dispute Settlement under GATT and the Tokyo Round Agreements, USITC Publication 1793 (Washington, D.C. 1985) 68, 70. For P. KALLA, The GATT Dispute Settlement Procedure in the 1980s: Where Do We Go From Here? Dickinson Journal of International Law 5 (1986) 82, 97, the U.S. only started to push for an adjudicating approach after the EEC and Japan became competitors in the field of trade.

36. ICJ Reports 1984, for the declaration of termination of 7.10.1985 of the U.S. acceptance of the compulsory jurisdiction of the ICJ cf. ILM 24 (1985) 1742. This termination has given rise to divided opinions which are referred to by K. HIGHET, "You Can Run But You Can't Hide"—Reflections on the U.S. Position in the Nicaragua Case, Virginia Journal of International Law 27 (1987) 551 et seq. with further references.

37. ICJ Reports 1984, 246.

38. See Section 301.

39. Reported by Agence Europe No. 4632 of Oct. 5/6, 1987, 10. The Agreement has been signed on Jan. 2, 1988.

40. For a detailed accoung cf. R.B. BILDER, When Neighbours Quarrel: Canada-U.S. Dispute-Settlement Experience, Disputes Processing Research Program, Working Papers Series 8, Institute for Legal Studies, University of Wisconsin (1987). BILDER reports that Chief Justice JAY later had been 'guillotined in effigy' as a traitor for his work on the treaty (p. 3) and that in 1979 the Joint Working Group of the Canadian and American Bar Association had proposed compulsory adjudication for disputes relating to any treaty enforced between the two countries (p. 5.).

41. JACKSON, supra n. 15, Crumbling Institutions 102.

42. Cf. BRONCKERS, supra n. 26, 167 et seq.

43. See HUDEC, supra n. 4, referring to GATT litigation for the purpose of constructing "political symbols back home."

44. In favour of binding DS arrangements cf. the Statement by an Expert Panel: U.S. Policy on the Settlement of Disputes in the Law of the Sea (Strasbourg 1986), American Journal of International Law 81 (1987), 438 et seq.

45. L.M. FRIEDMAN, Total Justice (Boston 1987).

46. FRIEDMAN, op. cit., refers to 650,000 practicing lawyers in the U.S.— ten times as many as in Japan. According to other sources there are only 12,000 licensed lawyers in Japan. In the case of the EC an estimate of 300,000 practicing lawyers may be realistic. For a balanced view as to the U.S. legal system and its handling of international trade affairs cf. J.H. JACKSON, Perspectives on the Jurisprudence of International Trade: Costs and Benefits of Legal Procedures in the United States, Michigan Law Review 82 (1984), 1570 et seq. See the reference

in FRIEDMAN, supra n. 45, 16, to J.K. LIEBERMAN, The Litigious Society (1981).

47. For details see FRIEDMAN, loc. cit., 39 et seq.

48. Cf. T. IGUCHI, Japan and the New Law of the Sea: Facing the Challenge of Deep Sea Mining, Virginia Journal of International Law 27 (1987), 527 et seq.

49. K. MATSUMOTO aims mainly at a higher persuasiveness of the panels within the GATT DS procedure, in Bilateral v. GATT Dispute Settlement, paper given to the London Conference of Sept. 14–18, 1987 of the International Bar Association, manuscript p. 15. According to the USITC-Report (1985), supra n. 35, 68, the greatest resistance against any DS reform under the Tokyo Round was on the part of the EEC and Japan; see also D.E. de KIEFFER, GATT Dispute Settlements: A New Beginning in International and U.S. Trade Law, Northwestern Journal of International Law and Business 17 (1980) 317, 321. According to Agence Europe No. 4638 of Oct. 14, 1987, 6, Japan will follow the panel report in the "Tax Regime For Alcoholic Beverages" Case before the report becomes final, as Japan "wants to be in line with the GATT dispositions."

50. According to HUDEC, supra n. 5, 152 developing countries are pressing for the strict enforcement of developed-country obligations. According to W. Benedek, The Participation of Africa in the General Agreement on Tariffs and Trade (GATT), Verfassung und Recht in Übersee 20 (1987) 45 et seq., it is the traditional African approach in international law to aim for consensus and conciliation in the settlement of disputes. Under GATT only Malawi once used the procedure under Art. XXII: see BISD 15S/116 et seq.

51. See M. Gorbachev, Reality and Guarantees for a Secure World, Information Service of the United Nations Association in the USSR, Oct. 1987, No. 4/21, 3 (6), underlining that the "mandatory jurisdiction [of the ICJ] should be recognized by all on mutually agreed conditions"; see also W.E. BUTLER, Judicial Settlement of Disputes in Russian International Legal Doctrine: The Legacy of L.A. KA-MAROSKII, Emory Journal of International Dispute Resolution 1 (1986) 33 et seq.; S.E. Samuels, The Soviet Position on International Arbitration: A Wealth of Choices or Choices for the Wealthy, Virginia Journal of International Law 26 (1986) 417 et seq.: The more traditional approach, rejecting the idea of a compulsory jurisdiction of the ICJ, is reflected by D.B. LEWIN, Das Prinzip der friedlichen Beilegung internationaler Streitigkeiten (Berlin 1980) 95 et seq.

52. According to I.H. COURAGE-van LIER, Supervision within the General Agreement on Tariffs and Trade, in P. van Dijk (ed.), Supervisory Mechanisms in International Economic Organizations (Deventer et al. 1984) 49, 200, indicating that until 1960 this creative function of the DS procedure was highly effective; with the decreasing cohesiveness in GATT the effectiveness of the creative function had declined.

53. For the conclusion of side agreements cf. JACKSON, supra n. 15, Crumbling Institutions 96 et seq.

54. Cf. GATT Activities 1986, 47, and the tabular list published in the Analytical Index, supra n. 6, under Art. XXIII -87 et seq.; HUDEC, supra n. 4 (manuscript p. 3), indicates that since 1948 over 130 GATT lawsuits have been initiated.

55. Cf. HUDEC, loc. cit.

56. This is at least the experience from the intense deliberations among the representatives of the governments of the twelve Member States in the Council of the EC.

57. Cf. JACKSON, supra n. 5, Governmental Disputes 5, 7 et seq.; HUDEC, supra n. 5, 171 et seq., and de LACHARRIÈRE, supra n. 16, 343 et seq.

58. Cf. McGOVERN, supra n. 5, 73 et seq.

59. K. OELLERS-FRAHM/N. WÜHLER, Dispute Settlement in Public International Law, Text and Materials (Berlin 1984). For an analytical overview of the area of international dispute settlement cf. R.B. BILDER, An Overview of International Dispute Settlement, Emory Journal of International Dispute Resolution 1 (1986) 1 et seq.; J.G. MERRILLS, International Dispute Settlement (London 1984), and the relevant contributions to Installment 1 on Settlement of Disputes, in R. BERNHARDT (ed.), Encyclopedia of Public International Law (Amsterdam et al. 1981).

60. For a more restrictive view see E. OESER, Zur Bedeutung von Verhandlungen im Völkerrecht, Neue Justiz 40 (1986) 84, 86, who recognizes only a general obligation to offer a possibility of contact ("Kontaktpflicht").

61. Cf. MERRILLS, supra n. 60, 1 et seq., 18.

62. Cf., however, the inductive approach of C. THUN-HOHENSTEIN, Konsultationen als Verfahren in den Internationalen Bezie-hungen (Wien 1983), and idem, Konsultationen: Versuch einer Klassifizierung, Austrian Journal of Public and International Law 35 (1984/85) 155 et seq., analyzing eight different types of consultations. For the advantages and disadvantages (impasse, element of power, influence of special pressure groups, issues of principle, absence of neutrally agreed upon facts or data) of the method of negotiation cf. BILDER, supra n. 60, 22 et seq.

63. Supra n. 55 et seq.

64. BILDER, supra n. 40, 34 et seq.

65. See MERRILLS, supra n. 60, 20 et seq.; a different terminology is proposed by R.L. BINDSCHEDLER, Conciliation and Mediation, in R. Bernhardt (ed.), Encyclopedia of Public International Law, Installment 1 (Amsterdam et al. 1981), 47 et seq. Bindschedler distinguishes mediation undertaken by states and conciliation offered by private persons. In both cases a third party intervenes in disputes between states with the purpose of contributing to their settlement.

66. For details see MERRILLS, loc. cit., 33 et seq.

67. For the different procedures see the report of M.K.M.K. YASSEEN, Les commissions internationales d'enquéte, Yearbook of the Institute of International Law, vol. 60 II (Paris 1983), 313 et seq.

68. Cf. MERRILLS, supra n. 60, 52 et seq. For the procedures under the Law of the Sea Convention see BERNHARDT, supra n. 12, and G. JAENICKE, Solutions for Dispute Settlement Procedures Elaborated by the Conference on the Law of the Sea, in K.-H. Böckstiegel (ed.), Settlement of Space Law Disputes (Köln et al. 1980), 113 et seq.

69. The most recent and detailed analysis is by R.B. BILDER, International Dispute Settlement and the Role of Adjudication, in L.F. DAMROSCH, The

International Court of Justice at a Crossroads (New York 1987) 155 et seq.; for the procedures of arbitration under the ICSID-Convention see in the following under n. 124.

70. Cf. Art. 42 of the Treaty Instituting the Benelux Economic Union of Feb. 3, 1958, see OELLERS-FRAHM/WÜHLER, supra n. 60, 415.

71. Cf. the decision of the CPs of March 3, 1955, in BISD 3S/13, para 20.

72. Cf. BISD 12S/65 referring to the terms of reference which requested the panel to "assist" the disputing parties by issuing an advisory opinion.

73. For the advantages and disadvantages of permanent tribunals and comparison to ad hoc arbitral tribunals see BILDER, supra n. 71, 162 et seq.; MERRILLS, supra n. 60, 88; H. MOSLER/R. BERNHARDT (eds.), Judicial Settlement of International Disputes (Berlin 1974), and H. STEINBERGER, Judicial Settlement of International Disputes, in R. Bernhardt (ed.), Encyclopedia of Public International Law, Installment 1 (Amsterdam et al. 1981), 120 et seq.

74. Art. 297 of the Convention; see the comment by G. JAENICKE, Dispute Settlement under the Convention of the Law of the Sea, ZaöRV 43 (1983) 813, 817 et seq.

75. See Art. 187 of the Law of the Sea Convention.

76. See Art. 290 of the Law of the Sea Convention.

77. See Art. 284 and Annex V, § 1, to the Convention.

78. Discussed by de LACHARRIÈRE, supra n. 16, 339 et seq., 350; cf. J. de ARECHAGA, The Amendments to the Rules of Procedure of the ICJ, American Journal of International Law 67 (1973), 1 et seq.

79. Cf. Art. 38 § 2 of the Statute of the ICJ of June 26, 1945 ("[p]ower of the Court to decide the case ex aequo et bono, if the parties agree thereto"). The ICJ has never based a decision on this provision, although it referred to the principle of equity in international law. For this see M.E. VILLIGER, Die Billigkeit im Völkerrecht: Neuere Entwicklungen in der Rechtsprechung und der Staatspraxis, Archiv des Völkerrechts 25 (1987) 174 et seq. Cf. also the references to equitable solutions in Art. 74, para. 1, and Art. 73, para. 1, of the Law of the Sea Convention. Cf. the flexible approach by H. Mosler, The Area of Justiciability: Some Cases of Agreed Delimitation in the Submission of Disputes to the International Court of Justice, in J. Makarczyk (ed.), Essays in International Law in Honour of Judge Manfred Lachs (The Haque et al. 1984) 409–421.

80. Cf. Arts. 93 et seq. of the Charter, and JACKSON, supra n. 5, World Trade 166 et seq.

81. It may be interesting to speculate, Why: In analyzing the cases decided by the two permanent courts, it appears that states were willing to submit cases which relate to more unique situations and which do not concern their ongoing and continuing relationships. States do settle these disputes normally by agreement which takes their continuing interdependencies into account. For further reasons see M. VIRALLY, Le champ opératoire du règlement judiciaire international, Revue général du droit international public 87 (1983) 281, 308 et seq.

82. ICJ Reports 1969, 3 et seq.; see in detail Mosler, supra n. 81, 409 et seq.

83. See P. PESCATORE, Introduction, in M. Hilf/F.G. Jacobs/E.-U. Petersmann (eds.), The European Community and GATT (Deventer et al. 1986) XV et seq.

84. Cf. Case 236/84, Mult GmbH, judgment of June 24, 1986, to be published, giving wide discretion to the EC Commission to handle complex economic matters. In regard to actions of Member States, the Court exercises strict control when the Member States act in the execution of Community law. The reason for this differentiated approach is the Court's task to guarantee the uniform application of Community law: cf. for example Case 184/83 HOFMANN (1984) ECR 3047, 3075 et seq.; cf. Art. 37 of the Statute of the CJEC (EEC).

85. See for example Art. 20 of the Statute of the CJEC (EEC).

86. Cf. Arts. 40 and 103 of the Rules of Procedure of the CJEC fixing time limits of one or two months depending on the specific procedure.

87. Art. 186 EEC Treaty; for a comparative analysis cf. K. OELLERS-FRAHM, Interim Measures of Protection in R. Bernhardt (ed.), Encyclopedia of Public International Law, Installment 1 (Amsterdam et al. 1981) 69 et seq.

88. It is true that under Art. 173 § 2 EEC Treaty individuals may attack only decisions which are addressed to them and are of direct and individual concern to the individual. In regard to acts of a more general nature, for example regulations or directives, individuals are not in a position to bring an action before the Court. They may, however, address themselves to the EC Commission, which under the procedure of surveillance (Art. 169 EEC Treaty) has a general obligation to bring matters before the CJEC which are not in conformity with the Treaty. This not formalized access of the individual to the EC Commission can be effective, although surprisingly it has been used frequently only in recent times.

89. Of different opinion is apparently COCCIA, supra n. 4, 42 et seq., advocating a binding effect of the panel decisions; in the case of sensitive matters contracting parties could make reservations.

90. For example by JACKSON during the Bielefeld Conference who emphasized that the fragmented procedures, as they are practiced at present, tend to damage the system, are hard to be understood by the public, and make it difficult for the parties to select the appropriate procedures.

91. For example Art. XXIV GATT; see JACKSON, supra n. 5, Governmental Disputes 9.

92. See supra n. 74 for the reference to the Case of the "Chicken-War."

93. A deterring example which demonstrates the risks of any differentiation is the DS procedure under the Subsidies Code. This more stringent procedure was attached to a Code on the substance of which there was not a large degree of consensus. Therefore, a number of procedures deadlocked and discredited the whole DS system; see HUDEC, supra n. 5, 183 and idem, supra n. 4.

94. Cf. Arts. 51 and 52 of the ICSID Convention (1965) opening a request for annulment of any award of the ICSID Tribunal. For various other models, all based on a system of reciprocity, cf. JACKSON, supra n. 5, Governmental Disputes 10 adhering, however, to a unitary and not fragmented procedure fearing otherwise increased disputes on procedures and less chances for developing a reliable case law.

95. A particular and apparently most efficient procedure is provided for by the Textile Surveillance Body (TSB) operating under the Multifibre Arrangement

which by its authority "comes down hard on violators": cf. HUDEC, supra n. 5, 168. For details of the rules on interim measures under Arts. 26 and 47 of the ICSID Convention see B.P. MARCHAIS, ICSID Tribunals and Provisional Measures, ICSID Review 1 (1986) 372 et seq.

96. In effect on 16./17.6.1987 the panel report in the "Super Fund-Case" was adopted by the GATT Council, thus concluding the entire procedure in only four months: Cf. GATT Newsletter FOCUS 48 (1987) 1.

97. See de LACHARRIèRE, supra n. 16, 341, referring to the Understanding of 1979 (para. 10). A recognized right is part of some of the Tokyo Codes, loc. cit., 345.

98. Cf. the Leutwiler Report, Welthandelspolitik für eine bessere Zukunft (Geneva 1985) 53. This report is discussed by de LACHARRIèRE, loc. cit., 347 et seq., who states with good reasons that such a reform would change completely the present DS machinery into a strictly judicial procedure.

99. De LACHARRIèRE suggests that in the future a contracting party should not be able to reject all of the panel members as proposed by the Director General, supra n. 16, 349.

100. Again de LACHARRIèRE, 351, favours a "concentration of choice" in respect to the panel members in order to arrive at a "homogeneous jurisprudence."

101. In the Annex to the Memorandum of 1979 it is reported that in most cases panels achieved their reports in a period of three to nine months: BISD 26S/235, 240 (1979) under No. 6 IX; however, the Subsidies Code provides for a period of sixty days after its establishment (Art. 18 para. 2) within which the panel "should" deliver its findings to the Subsidies Committee.

102. JACKSON, supra n. 5, Governmental Disputes 20, proposes that persons selected to sit on panels should prepare such a set of rules; for dissenting views see the Agreed Description of the Customary Practice of the GATT (1979) under 6 (I), BISD 26S/217.

103. According to No. 6 (IV) of the Agreed Description, loc. cit., panels may seek information from any relevant source they deem appropriate, consult experts to obtain their technical opinions, or seek advice or assistance from the Secretariat in its capacity as guardian of the General Agreement.

104. COCCIA, supra n. 4, 37, argues that the use of dissenting votes, as in the Pasta Panel Report of May 19, 1983 under the Subsidies Code, is an "invaluable feature of the common law tradition," a small step forward to a more "juridical" model of DS; also supra n. 104.

105. Emphasized by JACKSON on this conference; idem, supra n. 5, Governmental Disputes 5, 8, distinguishes the functions of conciliation, decision, rule or policy formulation, and recommendation or sanction. The panel decisions should lead to a body of "jurisprudence" that should orient the system: cf. JACKSON, supra n. 15, Crumbling Institutions, 104.

106. Cf. FLORY, supra n. 8, 343, referring to a number of panel reports which mention the principle of equity. For further reference to the principle of equity in jurisprudence within Public International Law cf. VILLIGER, supra n. 81, 174 et seq.

107. For a discussion of these questions see G. WEGEN, Vergleich und Klagerücknahme im internationalen Prozeß (Berlin 1987) 330, 333.

108. Cf. McGOVERN, supra n. 5, 79.

109. Cf. the Description of Customary Practice annexed to the Understanding (1979), BISD 26S/217. During the Bielefeld Conference Jackson stated that the notion "advisory opinion" is misleading and should be replaced by "provisional opinion" pending the decision of the GATT Council.

110. For the time being, the problem is not acute since GATT rules are not applied directly by national courts. J. TUMLIR, Conceptions of the International Economic and Legal Order, The World Economy 8 (1986) 87, describes the decisions of the CPs as being part of the executive's powers and are thus not able to bind the independent national judiciaries.

111. Cf. ROESSLER, supra n. 15, 44. For the "consensus minus two" cf. HUDEC, supra n. 1, giving the prognosis that this might be acceptable since it would not have to be paid by concessions on the substance (26 et seq.). Moreover, even the parties involved in a dispute would be able to find allies if they were forced to abstain or not to vote in the final deliberations of the CPs. FLORY, supra n. 8, 344, is opting for a majority vote of ⅔ or ⅗ or eventually ⅘ of the CPs.

112. Cf. Section 5 (Arts. 50 et seq.) of the ICSID Convention with respect to the Interpretation, Revision and Annulment of the Award. See also M.B. FELDMAN, The Annulment Proceedings and the Finality of the ICSID Arbitral Awards, ICSID Review 2 (1987) 85 et seq. For the International Civil Aviation Organization (ICAO) of Dec. 7, 1944 cf. Art. 86 on appeals against decisions of the Council see OELLERS-FRAHM/WÜHLER, supra n. 60, 489.

113. Cf. B.P. MARCHAIS, ICSID Tribunal and Provisional Measures, ICSID Review 1 (1986) 372, referring to rule 39 al. (5) of the Revised Arbitration Rules of Sept. 26, 1984 (ICSID/15, Basic Documents, January 1985) 80.

114. For a differentiated view cf. W. MENG, Streitbeilegung im GATT, ZaöRV 41 (1981) 69, 100 et seq. MENG admits that the exclusiveness has not been expressed in a clear GATT rule; if, however, the CPs cannot bring a dispute to a final solution, the contracting parties still have recourse to other measures under general public international law.

115. See JACKSON's proposal for a unified DS system which would apply to the overall GATT-MTN-Services System; also idem, supra n. 5, Governmental Disputes 13 et seq.

116. For further references cf. J.A. FROWEIN, Verpflichtungen erga omnes im Völkerrecht und ihre Durchsetzung, in R. Bernhardt et al. (eds.), Völkerrecht als Rechtsordnung, Internationale Gerichtsbarkeit, Menschenrechte, Festschrift für Hermann Mosler (Berlin a.o. 1983) 240, 255.

117. See the comment by J.P. HAYES, Conference on European-United States Trade Relations, Brussels 12./14.6.1986.

118. JACKSON on the Bielefeld II Conference.

119. See in particular the proposals of R. BLACKHURST in: PETERSMANN/HILF (eds.), The New GATT Round, supra n. 2, p. 123.

120. Cf. The GATT Negotiations and U.S. Trade Policy, The Congress of the U.S. Congressional Budget Office (Washington, D.C., 1987) XVII.

121. Discussed by JACKSON, supra n. 5, World Trade 187 et seq. and HILF, supra n. 26, 279 et seq. with further references.

122. Cf. ICSID Cases 1972–1987, ICSID/16/Rev. 1 (July 1987). By June 1987 89 states had ratified the Convention. See also E.F.E. SHIHATA, Toward a Greater Depolitization of Investment's Disputes: The Role of ICSID and MIGA, ICSID Rev. 1 (1986) 1 et seq.; G. Sacerdoti, La convenzione di Washington del 1965: Bilancio di un ventennio dell'ICSID, Rivista di diritto internazionale privato e processuale 23 (1987) 13 et seq.; S.K. Chatterjee, The Convention Establishing the Multilateral Investment Guarantee Agency, International Comparative Law Quarterly 36 (1987) 76 et seq.; and J. Voss, Die Multilaterale Investitionsgarantie-Agentur, Recht der Internationalen Wirtschaft 33 (1987) 89 et seq.

123. See PETERSMANN, supra n. 17, 64.

124. J.H. JACKSON/J.V. LOUIS/M. MATSUSHITA, Implementing the Tokyo Round (Ann Arbor 1984) 207 et seq., proposing a sort of filter as in the case of the European Convention on Human Rights; cf. also BRONCKERS, supra n. 26, 240 et seq.

125. Under para. 15 of the Understanding (1979), supra n. 6, the panels may seek information and technical advice from any individual or body, but only after having informed the government of the country in question.

126. One historical lesson for a pragmatic development regarding the access of individuals to an international DS system is the case of the European Convention on Human Rights. According to the original text of this Convention the complainant had no right to appear before the Court and to plead his case personally. Yet, the European Commission of Human Rights succeeded in involving the complainant in its pleadings before the Court by nominating the individual concerned as an "expert." The European Court of Human Rights reacted favourably in order to get more insight into the case by the personal appearance of the complainant. Finally, in 1982, the Rules of Procedures of the Court have been amended; see Art. 30 of the Rules of Procedure and the commentary of J.A. FROWEIN/W. PEUKERT, Europäische Menschenrechtskonvention, EMRK-Kommentar (Straßburg/Arlington 1985) 440, 559.

127. See JACKSON supra n. 2 and supra n. 15, Crumbling Institutions 93 et seq.

128. Cf. R. ROGOWSKI, Trade and Democratic Institutions, International Organization 41 (1987) 203 et seq.

129. The interrelationship of the quality of rules and the possible effects of any DS rules is emphasized by de LACHARRIÈRE, supra n. 16, 348 and by HUDEC, supra n. 5, 183, and idem, in Proceedings of the 74st Annual Meeting of the American Society of International Law (1980) 129, 134. See also E.-U. Petersmann, Constitutional Functions of Public International Economic Law, in P. van Dijk et al. (eds.), Restructuring the International Economic Order: The Role of Law and Lawyers (Deventer et al. 1987) 49 et seq.

130. See HUDEC, supra n. 20, 23, referring to the Subsidies Code under the Tokyo Round as an "international paper obligation" which is serving mainly for purposes of politics at home.

131. Single European Act of Feb. 17/28, 1986 (in force on July 1, 1987), Official Journal No. L 169/1 of June 29, 1987; cf. for the text of the European Parliament F. CAPOTORTI/M. HILF/F.G. JACOBS/J.-P. JACQUÉ, The European Union Treaty (Oxford 1986).

6

Prospects for the Uruguay Round: The Declaration of Punta del Este

Bernhard Zepter

In late 1986, the General Agreement on Tariffs and Trade (GATT) started a new round of multilateral trade negotiations, the so-called Uruguay Round. Launched in the Uruguayan town of Punta del Este in September 1986 and scheduled to last no more than four years, the Uruguay-Round negotiations address a comprehensive set of unresolved trade issues.

The Uruguay Round is the eighth round of multilateral trade negotiations since the establishment of the GATT in 1948. So far, the main objective of these rounds was to reduce average tariff rates on industrial products. Indeed, after seven rounds of negotiations, average tariffs in industrialized countries fell from over 40 percent in 1948 to about 5 percent in 1988. During the same period, the volume of international trade in manufactured goods increased dramatically, up to a figure 20 times that of 1948. At the same time, more and more countries became members of GATT. Today, GATT is a family of 96 countries. This represents a nearly fourfold increase over 1948. Even more countries can be regarded as de facto members. As for the People's Republic of China, it is currently negotiating its accession to the GATT. For its part, the Soviet Union has signaled its interest in joining it.

Today, in spite of these positive developments, the GATT system faces considerable problems which challenge its credibility and effectiveness. After a period of economic decline in the early 1980s, due mainly to structural macroeconomic imbalances as well as inadequate adjustments in the following years, protectionist pressures increased in many countries. Since then, there has been a growing number of attempts to bypass GATT through bilateral arrangements or to hamper free trade through nontariff measures or other measures of a discriminatory character. So-called "Voluntary Export Restrictions" (VERs) or "Orderly Market Arrangements" (OMAs), gray-area measures through which stronger traders often try to impose their specific economic interests, undermined free trade by making liberal use of the Most Favored Nation principle. At the same time, the claim for "fair trade" more often dissimulated a certain lack of willingness to "play the game" and to accept the rules of a free, liberalized market.

But part of the problem is the success story of GATT itself: The increased number of participants eroded the well established world leadership in trade. The system became more and more complicated, countries or groups of countries asked for special and differential treatment or excluded the application of specific rules and obligations with the argument that they were unacceptable at a given stage of their development. In some areas, markets were flooded with low-priced products as the result of economic policy practices like laser-beaming and industrial targeting. More often, governments both in developed and developing countries simply felt unable to undertake necessary but unpopular adjustment measures, thus not responding to the effects of increasing international competition.

As a result of these developments, temptation grew to seek bilateral or regional arrangements. Even the United States which for a long time fought such a tendency, recently signed free trade agreements with Israel and Canada. And it is currently giving serious thought to the possibility of engaging in similar agreements with Japan and Mexico and is holding talks with these countries about it. With constantly reduced tariff barriers and diminished opportunities to plan for their export or import policies, governments often looked for other nontariff possibilities to regulate their internal economic development. At the same time, in view of an increasingly open market, specific rules for fair competition were given more weight than before. This resulted in increased pressure, especially from countries with high standards, to develop or harmonize laws and regulations such as the protection of intellectual property rights and of labor and social rights in the field of domestic investment policies.

Against this background, the launching of trade negotiations in the framework of the Uruguay Round was of great importance. In the view of many participants, this new round of multilateral trade negotiations offers the possibility to restore the credibility of the multilateral trading system and to roll back domestic protectionist pressures. In general terms, the round aims at further liberalizing trade, strengthening the role of GATT, increasing GATT's responsiveness to developments in the international economic environment and fostering cooperative actions to improve the interrelationship between trade and other economic policies, thereby promoting growth and development.

In comparison with earlier rounds, the Uruguay Round is certainly the most ambitious of its kind. It goes beyond traditional issues like tariff or nontariff measures and tries to solve problems like agriculture, which in the past were largely neglected. The Uruguay Round is also aimed at re-establishing GATT rules and disciplines in sectors like textiles and clothing, where in the past markets have been relegated to special regimes. Rules and disciplines in the field of the protection of intellectual property rights, as well as in the context of national investment policies, should protect the rules of fair competition in a multilateral environment and remove unjustified barriers to trade. Moreover, the negotiations will seek to open new opportunities for trade in areas such as services.

Through a comprehensive set of negotiations, countries are trying to reform GATT as an institution. GATT matters should be given greater weight in global macroeconomic policy-making. In general, the role of trade in world economic and financial policy should be more fully recognized. For this purpose, closer cooperation with other international organizations, dealing with monetary and finance matters, ought to be established. The effectiveness of GATT's work should be enhanced by strengthening the role of the GATT secretariat and of the director general. A special surveillance mechanism should be created to increase transparency within GATT and to contribute to a greater mutual understanding of domestic trade policies and economic problems of individual member states.

A strengthened dispute settlement regime should encourage contracting parties to seek a multilateral settlement of their trade disputes and to refrain from unilateral actions.

For the purpose of the negotiations, ministers have established a Trade Negotiating Committee, or TNC, which generally meets on the level of high officials but—as in the case of the Midterm Review—also at the ministerial level. The TNC comprises two subsidiary bodies, the Group of Negotiations of Goods, or GNS, which supervises 14 different negotiating groups, and the Group of Negotiations on Services, or GNS, which deals exclusively with the new and particularly complicated issue of the liberalization of trade in services. During the negotiations, GATT members also committed themselves to apply a "standstill" and "rollback" policy concerning trade-distorting measures inconsistent with GATT obligations. A special surveillance body has been charged with the supervision of this commitment.

The Initial Phase of the Negotiations

The negotiations opened in 1987 with an "initial phase" which ended as scheduled in December 1987. During this phase, participants in the negotiations were asked to clarify among themselves the content and modalities of the negotiations, as well as to submit first proposals. Negotiators were invited to undertake every effort to move the Uruguay Round forward as quickly as possible and to achieve concrete results in all areas of negotiations.

The initial phase of the Uruguay Round provided an encouraging start to the negotiations. More than 90 sessions were organized and about 245 working documents introduced into the negotiations during this period. Despite differences in substance, the atmosphere of the negotiations was businesslike. At the end of the phase, there was broad agreement among participants that good progress had been made but that further substantial efforts were necessary to reach the final goal of Punta del Este.

The successful conclusion of the initial phase was followed by a smooth transition to the real negotiating phase. In 1988, negotiators concentrated on further specifying their proposals and started to discuss concepts and principles for possible agreements. After the summer break in 1988, participants started to prepare for the Midterm Review which took place at the ministerial level in Montreal on December 1988.

For the beginning, two different concepts marked the preparation of the Midterm Review: Whereas the United States and the group of so-called "fair traders in agriculture," the CAIRNS-Group, favored a substantial midterm negotiation with first conclusions and agreements ("early harvest") particularly in the field of agriculture, the European Community, Japan and most of the developing countries preferred a sort of "midterm rendezvous," comprising a ministerial assessment of the results achieved so far and more guidance on the part of the ministers as to further negotiations.

In preparation for the Montreal meeting, both sides finally met in an attempt to achieve as many concrete results as possible. The basis for this compromise was the principle of globality, confirmed explicitly by the ministers in the Punta del Este Declaration. This principle underlines the interrelationship between the different items of the Uruguay Round negotiations. As developing countries were pressing for early results and concrete offers in the field of tropical products (a claim based on the wording of the Punta del Este declaration), as the United States (for domestic policy reasons) was asking for substantial, future-oriented results in agriculture, and as the negotiations on the institutional issues were making steady progress, the respect of the principle of globality pre-supposed an overall balanced package of midterm conclusions in all areas of the Uruguay-Round negotiations.

Results of the Midterm Review

On this basis, the midterm package became much more ambitious than initially intended. Under great pressure of time, the ministers tried to advance in parallel all areas of the negotiations. In Montreal, it became apparent that the time for the preparation of the most disputed items, in particular in the field of agriculture, was too short. The ministers reached an agreement on 11 items but kept the results on hold pending resolution of four as yet unresolved problems on textiles, agriculture, safeguards and in the field of protection of trade-related intellectual property rights (TRIPS). The director general of the GATT, Arthur Dunkel, was charged by ministers to consult with individual delegations and to find room for compromise. In April 1989, the TNC met on the level of high officials in Geneva to examine Mr. Dunkel's findings. In this second midterm conference, final agreement was reached on the four items still open.

The successful conclusion of the Midterm Review represented considerable progress for the further work of the Uruguay Round negotiations. Although the progress achieved was uneven, the package was generally interpreted as a balanced and acceptable approach.

1. Both developed and developing countries offered a first set of concessions in the field of tropical products. The implementation of these measures is already under way. Developing countries expect further concessions at the end of the negotiations.

2. In the field of tariff and nontariff measures, participants committed themselves to further substantial tariff reductions to be agreed upon during the round and fixed some of the criteria for the elimination of nontariff measures. The question of whether reductions should be achieved through a request-and-offer procedure or through a general formula (like in the Tokyo Round) was left open, but reaching a final agreement by the end of the negotiations should not be too much of a problem.

3. In the particularly sensitive field of agriculture, substantial progress was achieved. Participants agreed on a short term freeze in the overall support level for agricultural products and committed themselves to a first reduction ("down payment") of these levels, counting from the beginning of the negotiations in September 1986. As to the long term goals of the negotiations, participants agreed to establish a fair and market-oriented agricultural trading system, thereby taking into account the interests of the net importing countries, as well as more operationally effective GATT rules and principles.

The TNC finally accepted the formula that the long-term objective of the agricultural negotiations was to provide for substantial progressive reductions in agricultural support and to sustain protection over an agreed period of time. Although the United States refrained from its initial request to aim at the "elimination," not only the "reduction," of support measures, the European Community had considerable misgivings about this formula, as it limits decisively its room for maneuver in the context of the Common Agricultural Policy. Moreover, specific rules and principles will be defined for questions like import access, subsidies and support measurements and with respect to the role of the developing countries.

4. The conclusions in textiles and clothing were successful only to a lesser extent. This item eventually turned out to be among the most difficult ones dealt with at the midterm meeting. In particular the European Community had serious difficulties in accepting a clear and binding commitment for the phase-out of the Multi Fibre Agreement (MFA). Textile producing developing countries have sought for many years the opening of textile markets according to GATT rules. Since 1961, when for the first time 19 countries concluded a special market arrangement on textiles outside GATT, trade in textiles and clothing has been regulated under an MFA regime which at a later stage grew to include many more countries. Developing countries have requested the phase-out of the MFA and the re-establishment of the Most Favored Nation principle of the GATT in this area of particular interest to them.

The ministers finally agreed that modalities for the process of integration of the textile sector into GATT should cover the phase-out of restrictions under the MFA and other restrictions on textiles and clothing inconsistent with the GATT rules and disciplines. In "substantive negotiations," participants will seek to fix the time span of such a process, which should commence following the conclusion of negotiations in 1990. In accepting this formula, developed countries like the European Community have finally agreed to gradually phase out the MFA, starting in 1991. Although the modalities of this process are not yet agreed, developing countries can consider this commitment as a major breakthrough in their fight against the MFA.

5. In close connection with the textile and clothing sector, another important item is causing considerable problems to the negotiators of the Uruguay Round: the particularly sensitive item of GATT safeguards. Article XIX of the General Agreement allows for derogations from the obligations of the GATT in specific, well defined cases. Contracting parties calling on GATT safeguards have to pay compensation. According to basic GATT principles, ordinary safeguard measures can only be applied on a nondiscriminatory basis, i.e. against all other Contracting Parties. In practice, this requirement turned out to be more and more circumvented as ever more countries asked for and were accorded special

and differential treatment. This development undermined the principle of the balance of rights and obligations in the GATT, which was the basic rationale behind the safeguard mechanism of the GATT. At the same time, developed countries looked for bilateral and selective mechanisms to cope with the problem of market disruption in trade among themselves.

The answer was the aforementioned gray-area measures like VERs and OMAs, taken in particular by large trading entities like the EC or the United States. As they were concluded on a voluntary basis, nobody really contested their "GATT ability." Some developing countries accepted the special arrangements as they guaranteed export quotas which—under the rules of open competition—were not necessarily available. The practice satisfied those who preferred a regulated market to the cold wind of free competition. On the other hand, it undermined basic GATT rules by introducing the notion of selectivity and bilateralism.

In light of the experience gained through the growing application of gray-area measures, an overwhelming majority of developing countries are pressing today for a reform of the GATT safeguard regime and for a return to the basic GATT principles. Developed countries like those of the European Community generally do not contest the need for reform but want to preserve the principle of selectivity in some form, at least temporarily. In return, they want to see more integration of developing countries, in particular the newly industrialized countries (NICs), into the GATT discipline. They are also waiting for the development in areas like textiles and agriculture, where gray-area measures seem particularly important to preserve their basic economic interests.

Owing to these circumstances, the midterm meeting could not yet produce definite results. Again, the ministers stressed the importance of the issue and, in rather general terms, stated their readiness to seek the re-establishment of multilateral controls over safeguards. The chairman of the group, Ambassador Maciel from Brazil, was invited to draw up a draft text of a comprehensive agreement as a basis for negotiations. Mr. Maciel, meanwhile, has submitted such a draft proposal to the group.

6. As regards two more technical items, the further elaboration and expansion of the Tokyo Codes (MTN Agreements and Arrangements) as well as the area of Subsidies and Countervailing Measures, Ministers established a specific work program for further negotiations. These sectors may be technically complicated but should—maybe with the exception of the Antidumping Code, where developing countries complain about an excessive use of antidumping measures—cause lesser problems for the final overall conclusion of the Uruguay Round. In the area of

subsidies, however, a distinction has to be made with respect to other issues under consideration, e.g., agriculture.

7. Another sensitive topic at the Midterm-Meeting was the sector of Trade Related Aspects of Intellectual Property Rights (TRIPS). The developed countries advocated a GATT agreement to reduce distortions of, and impediments to, legitimate trade, caused by—in their view—inadequate standards of protection and enforcement of intellectual property rights (IPRs). The agreement should be based on appropriate standards for IPR protection, drawing from international conventions or, if necessary, national laws. It should also include provisions for the application of basic GATT principles such as national treatment and transparency, both internal and border enforcement measures and a dispute-settlement mechanism, according to relevant GATT provisions.

Most developing countries contested the competence of GATT to deal with IPR norms and standards, as they were dealt with in other international forums, in particular in the World Intellectual Property Organization, or WIPO. But they declared themselves ready to negotiate a GATT code on counterfeiting and to examine the relevance of existing GATT rules and principles for IPR protection. For two years, these basic differences caused a deadlock in the negotiations. The midterm meeting finally succeeded in breaking it: the ministers agreed that the TRIPS negotiations should encompass the provision of adequate standards and principles concerning the availability, scope and use of TRIPS as well as the provision of effective and appropriate means for the enforcement of these rights. In response to specific concerns raised by developing countries, agreement was reached that consideration would be given to the underlying public policy objectives of respective national IPR systems, including developmental and technological objectives.

This compromise formula offers a fair chance for substantive negotiations in the TRIPS field. Developing countries have implicitly recognized the need to respond to a further opening of markets in developed countries by improved protection of IPR. Developed countries, in return, are ready to accept developmental and technological policy objectives in national IPR systems.

8. In the area of Trade Related Investment Measures (TRIMS), one of the three "new items" for negotiations in the GATT, the ministers agreed on a directive for further negotiations which confirmed the mandate of Punta del Este. They added a general obligation to include specific development aspects in the negotiations.

Negotiations in this area are aimed at reducing or eliminating investment measures with trade distorting effects, such as local content obligations, export performance, licensing requirements, manufacturing limitations or local equity obligations. They are still in a rather preliminary stage. This reflects considerable reluctance on the part of governments, also in developed countries, to reduce their freedom of action in the field of economic policy planning by, among other things, eliminating trade related investment measures like local content obligations or investment promoting. The main focus of the negotiations is therefore on the interpretation of existing GATT obligations, with the aim to further cutting down tendencies for abuse of TRIMS.

9. In the field of institutional reform of the GATT, i.e., Functioning of the GATT and Dispute Settlement, the ministers had to decide on a whole set of substantial proposals from the negotiating groups. They established a Trade Policy Review Mechanism (TPRM) which calls for regular reports of contracting parties on the main events and developments of their trade policies and practices. On the basis of these reports, contracting parties within the GATT should gain a better understanding of economic developments and objectives of individual member states. The assessment to be carried out under the TPRM will take place against the background of the wider economic and developmental needs of individual member states as well as their external environment. Upon request, the GATT secretariat will provide technical assistance to less developed contracting parties. The information contained in the specific country reports should be coordinated with notifications made under already existing GATT provisions.

The ministers also decided on a greater ministerial involvement in the GATT and agreed to meet at least once every two years for regular meetings of the contracting parties. They invited the director general of the GATT to approach the heads of the IMF and the World Bank to explore ways and means of achieving greater coherence in global economic policy-making through strengthening the relationship of GATT with other international organizations.

The ministers also took substantive decisions for improving the GATT dispute-settlement regime. These decisions range from an overall shortening of the time span for procedures, to precision in the consultation process, to expansion of the practices for good offices, to conciliation and mediation, to the introduction of the possibility of arbitration, and to specific changes in GATT-panel procedures. They include improvements in the establishment of a panel or a working party, in the application of standard terms of reference, the composition of a panel, the procedures for multiple complaints, the time devoted to various phases of a panel, and the adoption of panel reports.

As with the TPRM, the new regulations in the dispute-settlement procedures will be applied on a trial basis until the end of the Uruguay Round. Further improvements, in particular in connection with the surveillance and implementation of panel recommendations and rulings still need to be negotiated by the end of the round. By taking these far-reaching institutional decisions in Montreal, the trade ministers gave a clear signal of their determination to strengthen the GATT and to render its procedures more reliable and attractive.

10. In Montreal, considerable progress was also achieved in the most important of the new subjects, the progressive liberalization of trade in services. The negotiations in this area result from a long and controversial discussion on the future of world trade. Especially in developed countries, services account for a steadily increasing share of the national product. Modern services are highly innovative and in general know-how intensive. They are recognized as contributing considerably to the economic development of countries.

There are two types of services: First, traditional services like banking, insurance or transport which are largely regulated and therefore difficult to harmonize internationally. Second, new types of services like computer services, new telecommunications services, franchising or consulting which so far are subject to less regulation and governmental attention and which are expanding rapidly. They might be easier to liberalize than the traditional services.

From the standpoint of the developing countries, a distinction could be made between services like construction, tourism or some professional services, all of which are little dependent on emerging technologies, and those which presuppose access to large capital resources or high technology. In the latter case, developing countries might be competitive to a lesser extent, although some of the NICs are high performancers also in more sophisticated services.

As far as trade in services is concerned, there are still few experiences as to how liberalization could proceed in practice. In 1961, the OECD Council adopted the Codes on Liberalization of Current Invisible Operations and on Capital Movement. These codes are under constant review and were amended frequently. The United States has concluded free trade agreements with Israel and Canada, which include provisions for trade in services. Australia and New Zealand recently signed a similar agreement. The European Community also has considerable experience since the harmonization of trade in services is part of its efforts to create a single market by the end of 1992.

Despite this knowledge, multilateral coverage of trade in services is still practically nonexistent. Arrangements within the OECD do not necessarily reflect the realities of multilateral trade agreements according to GATT principles, but rather the interests of "like-minded" countries. Bilateral or free zones arrangements do not offer appropriate guidance as they respond to specific regional interests and are embedded in other, not even necessarily economic national policy objectives.

To a large extent, Uruguay Round negotiations on services are innovative and open up new dimensions of international economic relations. They are intellectually stimulating and complicated at the same time. From the beginning, the Group on Services (GNS) had to face considerable problems: A clear-cut definition of trade in services was neither available nor could the GNS base its discussions on reliable statistics and experience in the negotiating techniques for an agreement on services.

However, the negotiations on services have been more substantive and have proceeded faster than initially expected by many countries. Developing countries, which at the beginning of the round showed considerable reluctance to commit themselves in these negotiations, began to discover and to define their own interests and participated seriously in the process. In Montreal, the ministers succeeded in drawing first conclusions for general rules and concepts of a future agreement in services, including principles like transparency, national treatment, MFN and market access.

More important still, the ministers gave guidance for the way in which negotiations should be conducted: negotiation of concepts and principles of a future framework agreement on the basis of the Montreal conclusions, testing of sectors with a view to add sectorial annotations to these concepts, negotiation of effective market access to individual sectors on the basis of the principle of progressive liberalization. In principle, no sector should be excluded from the negotiations. Due account should be taken of developmental considerations, too.

Future Developments

Quite a number of uncertainties may influence further developments in the Uruguay Round. The fate of these negotiations depends not only on the good will of the negotiators but also on the various imponderables of global political and economic developments. So far, the talks have proceeded quite smoothly, and considerable progress has been made. In comparison with the Tokyo Round, the Uruguay Round negotiations have produced much more substance in the first two and a half years.

The negotiations have contributed to create a better climate in world trade, despite an increase in dispute settlement procedures at the beginning of the round. The fact that more disputes were brought before the GATT also reflects a growing confidence in the judicial power of the organization. The negotiations, together with the standstill commitment, exert considerable political pressure on the participants to refrain from unilateral action and to resist domestic protectionist pressure. With respect to rollback, only two offers have been tabled so far—by the EC and Japan.

Most participants expect rollback to be achieved toward the end of the Uruguay Round, as a result of a package rather than ahead of it unilaterally.

Concerning the individual items of the round, the ground is partially prepared for substantive conclusions and the future exchange of concessions. But there is no room for complacency. Although the Montreal package was generally balanced, progress in individual groups has been uneven and wide divergences of views continue to prevail.

As to agriculture, for example, a crucial issue for a number of countries, negotiations on the terms of achieving the ultimate long-term goals will be extremely difficult and heavily "politicized." The EC has already underlined its limited room for maneuver, as the common agricultural policy is the backbone of the balance of interests within the Community. Various considerations in the field of social, cultural or environmental policies and with respect to public health, security and consumer protection have to be taken into account and must be duly reflected in the agreement. A large number of developing countries profit from cheap food supplies through highly subsidized agricultural production in countries like those of the EC.

Agriculture is therefore one of those areas where negotiators generally do not expect a final result but rather the beginning of a process of liberalization, which will still require considerable efforts and time after conclusion of the Uruguay Round.

The same should be expected in the area of services. Nobody can seriously expect the final conclusion of results in this sector in the course of the round. The EC and other participants aim at a general framework agreement with sectoral annotations and a first package of liberalization measures in specific sectors of services as the result of the Uruguay Round. In the light of the difficulties ahead, this objective looks rather ambitious but should be achievable. So far, it has already become clear that the Uruguay Round negotiations have started a new process in this important area and that GATT members would be well advised to jump on the train before it leaves the station. Otherwise it might prove considerably more difficult to join the development. Countries which will adhere at a later stage to a services agreement will certainly have to pay a specific prize. Developing countries seem to have understood this message.

There are other highly sensitive areas where agreement will be difficult to achieve. Certainly, assessing the rules and the outcome of the final bargaining is still premature. But the contours of a final package are more apparent today than at the beginning of the negotiations. The principle of globality combines the different sectors to one single undertaking, although in some areas with graduation as to their importance. At this stage of the negotiations, the picture might be seen as follows.

The conclusion of the negotiations in the field of safeguards will largely depend on the overall substance of the final package. Clear rules and regulations concerning items like textiles and agriculture may lead to concessions by those countries which still consider selectivity and gray-area measures as being indispensable for the preservation of their interests. In the area of TRIPS, developed countries expect considerable efforts on the part of developing countries in exchange for further concessions in the field of market access. Developing countries cannot expect the further opening of markets and closer economic interlinkages if they do not respect basic rules of fair competition, one of them being the protection of appropriate IPR rights. On the other hand, developed countries should take concerns and problems of developed countries in this area seriously and respond to them appropriately, in particular through technical assistance.

The strengthening of the GATT through adequate institutional reforms is certainly not subject to "bargaining." It is in the interest of all contracting parties, particularly smaller countries. Requests from developing countries for special and more favorable treatment in this area are therefore inappropriate and counterproductive. A strengthened GATT regime for dispute settlement and an adequate solution of the problem of IPR protection will increase the pressure on the United States to refrain from unilateral action such as "super 301" and to accept a multilateral dispute-settlement regime.

Some of the items seem to be more at the periphery but are nevertheless important in the global equation as they reflect the interests of smaller or less influential groups of countries. This is true for the negotiations on tropical products or the natural resource-based products. In other areas like subsidies, nontariff measures or GATT articles, which largely overlap with some of the sensitive areas, agreements might be easier once these areas are settled.

Finally, the overall political and economic developments and conditions will decide on the outcome of the negotiations at the end of 1990. So far, all delegations have shown their willingness to achieve the objectives of Punta del Este. But uncertainties remain: The U.S. administration continues to be under protectionist pressures from Congress and is obliged by its trade law to carry out 301 measures which are not in conformity with GATT rights and obligations. The EC is preparing for its single market and might be tempted to concentrate its efforts on this important objective. The NICs might be reluctant to meet the request for more integration into GATT. Others might wish to prolong the negotiations for various reasons: to keep pressure on the EC until 1992, to avoid concessions or to reject unsatisfactory results. Major trading powers might prefer bilateral solutions instead of a multilateral approach.

But so far, these concerns do not seem justified. Most recently the EC decided to invite the trade ministers to meet in Brussels at the end of November 1990 for the concluding conference of the Uruguay Round. In doing so, the Community has underlined its commitment to a successful conclusion of the negotiations.

7

GATT: Revival or Decay?
A Plea for a New Transatlantic
Leadership Effort

Reinhard Rode

Estimating the future development of the GATT regime is necessarily guesswork. To be sure, the outcome of the Uruguay Round will be a test case for the prospects of the regime. But our question goes well beyond that. The very capacity of GATT to function as a liberal trade regulator is at stake.

The good midterm results of the Uruguay Round are cause for optimism as regards a successful outcome of this negotiation. Textiles, agriculture, safeguards and intellectual property rights are as many issues where room for compromise can be found. Since all negotiating parties need a successful conclusion to the talks, the Uruguay Round will very likely go down in the history of GATT as a success story, whether it produces substantive results or merely symbolic ones. Particularly as regards the sensitive issue of rising worldwide protectionism, none of the major participants in the round want to be blamed as GATT's gravedigger. This, however, is not the kind of posture on which GATT will thrive; it can only ensure its survival. Prospects for a further liberalization of world trade seem gloomy. While the cheerful message of a "successful" outcome of the Uruguay Round might satisfy the negotiators and some of the governments involved, liberal economists and the traders themselves are likely to find little of substance to applaud in it.

In all likelihood, the verdict on the Uruguay Round will resemble the one passed on the Omnibus Trade and Competitiveness Act of 1988 in the United States, which, although it actually strengthened the instruments of the protectionists, was sold politically as a liberalizing piece of legislation, as things might have been worse. Given the circumstances, from the institutional point of view, the outcome of the

Uruguay Round will not be all that bad since no showdown between the big traders and no North-South clash will have occurred. Certainly, this will have to be regarded as a success for all players and for GATT itself.

But what will this mean in the long term? First and foremost, the GATT regime will have bought time for restructuring. The Uruguay Round clearly shows that the negotiation business continues to function, thereby bearing witness to the survivability of the GATT regime under conditions of an eroded leadership role on the part of the United States. Ultimately, too, it will have demonstrated that the former liberal hegemon and initiator of all GATT rounds was able to carry on successfully with his role as the regime's driving force because no other major actor wanted to oppose it or dared do so. So much for the rosy picture. But again, what about trade liberalization? The United States has abandoned his role as the standard-bearer of liberal trade, and neither Japan nor the European Community with its forthcoming single market has seemed ready to assume it. There is no longer an eager stimulator of liberal trade, just three reluctant liberalizers. The former standard-bearer has come under increasing pressure from the advocates of protectionism at home; Japan has not yet converted to the free trade philosophy; and the European Community has turned inward, fully absorbed in the mechanics of bringing about its single market. Three "nonleaders" need not be such a bad thing for GATT in a time of transition, provided one can entertain realistic hopes of a fresh liberal stimulus, at least for the midterm. For now, the three main trading blocs, or free trade zones, the European Community, the United States and Canada, and to a lesser degree Asia, could serve as incubators for internal trade growth and, in the longer term, for fresh and globally-oriented liberalizing forces.

This might occur, and again it might not, and certainly must not. The optimistic scenario of a fruitful period of transition is based on the liberal belief that the positive effects of a global division of labor and free trade are so obvious that they ought to outweigh any negative effects of restrictive forces. It also posits that, in the long run, large traders cannot but favor free trade—if they pursue rational policies. Policymakers in the three main trading blocs, however, do not seem to want to make this kind of economic textbook wisdom theirs. Should their restrictive views prevail, they will act as a brake on the enlightened idea and practice of free trade. This faction sees its influence bolstered by opponents of the liberal trade principle in developing and newly industrializing countries, and by the de facto adversaries of this principle in the trading countries with centrally planned economies. And all of these countries are in various stages of their final accession to the GATT. Even if the small trading countries do not really matter in world trade in terms of volume, they do matter in terms of the GATT process. Since GATT has no such thing as a trade-weighted vote similar to the monetary strength-related vote in the IMF, the possibility of an unholy alliance of all of these free trade opponents cannot be dismissed out of hand. All of these players want something from GATT but are not willing to foot the liberal bill or contribute anything to the common cause of world trade. Absent a liberal leader, a gang of free riders may attempt to jettison GATT's discipline and to undermine the regime's liberal core. This sounds like doomsday for trade liberalization, and it is indeed a worst-case scenario. Such an outcome would verify the hegemonic stability theory that, without a strong liberal leader, meaning the United States, there can be no such thing as an effective free trade-oriented GATT regime; in other words, GATT's decay would be preprogrammed.

A more plausible scenario might be one of regime change under posthegemonic conditions. Under such a scenario, the free trade argument would come under fire and emerge weakened while that favoring a new role for GATT as a broker in matters of world trade would be strengthened. This, in turn, would lead to a greater acceptance of organized trade, or, for those who dislike the term "organized," "more managed" trade, which does not ring much better in free traders' ears, but suggests a somewhat lesser degree of regulation. On the agenda, however, is not the management of trade itself but that of trade conflicts. The latter has nothing to do with state trading but a lot with a platform for dispute settlement and reconciliation of trade conflicts, and with rules and procedures. Trade-conflict management has to be more than the mere implementation of free trade rules and penalization of those who break them, an approach that is not practicable anyway, owing to the lack of a liberal and effective rule-enforcing body. To the true liberal trade believers among economists, a Geneva-based trade-brokering GATT, empowered to negotiate and even to auction quotas, would be tantamount to an instrument forged by the devil in the furnace of hell. For a considerable period of time, however, such an instrument might very well meet the demands of world trade between relatively open economies in a far more satisfactory manner than the current liberal agreement, whose rules are being increasingly flaunted by some major GATT players and by most of the peripheral ones in the regime, too.

It is beyond question that the free trade idea lost momentum as the hegemonic power—the United States—withdrew its support. And the international body of liberal economists, its strong influence on GATT at the bureaucracy level notwithstanding, is not powerful enough to act as a substitute for the former hegemon. This, however, is far less a catastrophe for world trade than textbook wisdom would have it. During the 1980s, world trade continued to grow despite rising protectionism.

There is no reason to believe that this will not go on. On the global scale, important components of trade never abided by the free trade principle. For example, sectoral exceptions in the areas of agriculture, raw materials and textiles, among other things, and regional exceptions like North-South trade and East-West trade always existed. This is why we are faced not so much with the question of the overall level of world trade and growth prospects as we are with that of costs. Trade growth under protectionist or managed conditions cannot avoid the costs of protectionism; and this means higher prices for consumers. On the whole, economic textbooks are right when they say that protectionism and organized trade inevitably make the world poorer. But in the real world, the distribution of costs and, under free trade conditions, of benefits does not take place in an even or equitable manner, but favors some countries or regions over others. And there is the rub. And this is also why the world of the trade negotiators happens to be the real trade world, not that of liberal economists.

All of this is not to say that the goal of free trade is no longer worth pursuing. To the contrary, finding the best possible solution to achieve this goal, not crafting second- or third-best policies, is a matter of the utmost urgency, not some utopia. Free trade still makes sense and is, rightly, a short-, mid- and long-term goal of international trade politics. It should prevail as the dominant GATT principle. But this does not preclude that the trade world can live with different levels of trade openness. In my view, under conditions of a nonhegemonic trade system, one actually has no choice but to accept free trade areas and different levels of more or less free trade among various regions. Why shouldn't we accept the given reality of a broad scale of world trade ranging from free to organized, and, in the long run, try to improve on its more organized parts without adopting a uniform globalist approach?

Since free trade can only take place within free trade areas, instead of being denounced as trade fortresses, shouldn't the forthcoming EC single market and the U.S.-Canadian free trade area be hailed as examples worth imitating? In fact, the transatlantic trade area, cradle and locus of a once-flourishing GATT, remains the undisputed number one in the world of free trade. And this remains true despite the numerous U.S.-EC quarrels. Here is the area for which the free trade blueprint was made and where the actual practice of free trade came closest to the liberal principle. Within GATT and bilaterally, the United States and the European Community have set an extremely positive example of a trade-opening process. Provided transatlantic trade policy can be de-politicized, there is no reason why this successful free trade relationship should not be maintained and even expanded. The current U.S.-EC trade dispute should not be overrated: for all the posturing and the bluster, both sides are merely trying to introduce new if ever-weaker bargaining chips into the negotiation.

This is the trade area where the highest degree of economic integration has been achieved. Transatlantic trade is relatively balanced, intra-company trade is predominant, direct investment patterns are fairly symmetric and the open trade philosophy is more pronounced here than anywhere else in the world. Trade frictions, which stem from the overwhelming influence of agricultural policies on both sides of the Atlantic, are essentially a problem of parochial thinking within the U.S. Congress on the one hand and the EC Commission on the other. Were the United States to abandon its irresponsible attempts to scuttle the EC's Common Agricultural Policy and to declare itself satisfied with mutual reductions in agricultural subsidies—which would save both sides a lot of money anyway—this traditionally contentious issue could be defused and eventually settled. As for the European Community, it should lift some of its restrictions and open a fair share of its market to U.S.-made high-tech products, particularly in the area of telecommunications.

If there is a political lesson to be learned by the U.S. Congress and the Bush administration, it is that the United States must accept the relative balance in transatlantic trade and that it cannot misuse the European Community as a potential market for offsetting the huge imbalances to its detriment in transpacific trade. As a quid pro quo, the European Community could accept the United States as a player in the negotiating process that will ultimately lead to the establishment of a single European market three years from now. In light of the high degree of interdependence between the United States and the European Community, such a move would simply make sense, especially since it can be entirely ruled out that the United States would let itself be used as a Trojan horse by all the small outside traders. The big and open traders' common, legitimate and overriding interest is to manage their own affairs as freely as possible within the GATT framework. If the global reach of the concept known as Most Favored Nation, or MFN, has suffered somewhat in the process (and will continue to suffer), this must be seen as an acceptable and necessary price. In view of the fairly high number of free riders (for the most part in Asia), the wisdom of MFN rules ought to be questioned anyway. Such rules only make sense if the hegemon can easily assume the burden of nondiscriminatory behavior vis-à-vis weaker partners, or if relative homogeneity of trade behavior is predominant. Big and rich free riders necessarily make MFN rules look absurd and cannot but spur the demand for reciprocity and selectivity.

The transpacific trade area is the second most important trade area. Despite the high (and still growing) volume of trade taking place here, the level of trade integration in this area does not compare with that of the transatlantic area. First of all, only the United States abides by the liberal trade principle; its Asian partners have not yet fully converted to the economic precepts of Adam Smith and David Ricardo. Whether the Asian trading nations, in particular Japan and the four tigers, will eventually acquiesce in the liberal trade principle (meaning a balanced import-export behavior) or retain some or most of their free rider characteristics is an open question. Japan remains mainly an exporter of industrial products and an importer of raw materials, with deep-rooted cultural and societal obstacles hindering purchase and distribution of finished foreign products in accordance with the rules of comparative advantage. Thus the burden of adaptation rests squarely on Japanese shoulders. The world's most successful exporter (in terms of growth) must now prove it can be a fair importer, too, or face ever-escalating retaliatory measures on the part of the United States. Unless the Asian nations can be induced to co-operate by an array of carrots, which at any rate remains preferable to the blunt stick of escalating trade sanctions, it will prove impossible to implement in this area the relatively open rules of transatlantic trade. There is some hope yet that Japan may opt for the liberal trade path. Whether it does so fast enough remains to be seen.

Although Euro-Pacific trade is far lower in volume than transpacific trade, it faces essentially the same problems. Unless Japan increases its imports of finished European goods on the transatlantic pattern of intra-industry trade, the European Community will not hesitate to wield the stick of trade war and to impose quotas on Japanese goods in order to keep Japan from shipping some of its surplus production to Europe. Here, too, the choice is Japan's.

The intrapacific trade zone is the area where the mercantilists of the world are truly among themselves. Trade growth here has not been accompanied by much liberalization of commerce, at least until now. Also, since Japan, the leading country in the area, buys only relatively few finished products—despite their lower costs—from the small tigers, prospects for a regional free trade zone here are not too bright as yet. Should the Asian trading nations, with their policy of restricting regional industrial trade, squander further opportunities for growth, they are bound to become world champions in the quota business. Although they might eventually open up, the transition period is likely to be very long, for the necessary process of adaptation of will require far-reaching societal change.

For quite some time yet, North-South trade is expected to remain somewhat less than free, for developing countries need preferential treatment. While experience has shown that in most cases such treatment does little, if anything, to accelerate their economic development, they do have a right to ask for it. For most of these countries, the most urgent task is to remain in the world trade system at all, not to play the game of liberal trade. Failure to remain in the system would result in their becoming a group of small and insignificant traders.

The problems of East-West trade are similar to those of North-South trade. Countries with centrally planned economies are perforce nonliberal traders, whose aim is countertrade. As long as their currencies remain nonconvertible, thus depriving them of any real purchasing power, these countries will retain their status of potentially large markets. The issue of nonconvertibility is high on the Eastern reform agenda, with no resolution expected any time soon. East-West trade will remain a pretty thin slice of world trade for quite some time yet. For the Eastern bloc countries, acceding to GATT will be little more than a symbolic step and certainly no substitute for the ability to offer attractive and competitive products in the world marketplace. But economic reforms in the liberal mold and participation in GATT also mean that some Eastern countries will step up their efforts to join the world trade system. The attractiveness of the forthcoming EC single market has increased the pressure on East European countries to adapt and open up out of fear of falling back even further for the sake of preserving a closed and stagnating socioeconomic system.

Different levels of openness in the global trade system is a reality the GATT has to cope with. Accommodating these various levels can only be done incrementally, for overplaying one's hand at the liberal game would only result in disappointment and frustration. The GATT regime faces tremendous opportunities for opening the exchange of goods and services. Using these to the fullest, however, is contingent on acknowledging the respective differences in capability and will, and on treating them as existing subsystems with various speeds in their improvement possibilities.

This leads me to the conclusion that there exists a demand for a qualified system of differentiation and graduation within GATT. The respective shares of trade and the level of openness should be the yardstick of this system. To respond to the discrimination argument, let it be said that it just does not make sense for the top group of the relatively free and open Atlantic traders not to form their own dynamic subgroup within GATT. The regime ought to meet their specific demands since they are the only ones with the ability and the will to play the active role of liberalizers. The good example they would set might conceivably have some sort of public-relations effect and spur the other GATT members into following their lead. The highly integrated large Atlantic traders must be allowed to manage their own affairs to the best of their ability and in the interest of an optimum at open trade within GATT. To be sure, a GATT evolving into some UNCTAD-like platform would sooner or later become all but insignificant. The hope of the institutionalists that GATT is strong enough to stabilize itself will remain mere wishful thinking as long as the majority of its members do not partake of the liberal trade principle. This principle can only survive and flourish if the large traders themselves regard it as a goal worth pursuing and behave accordingly, i.e., in a liberal way. Who else but the United States and the European Community is better equipped to perform this task? Either they do it jointly or GATT will evolve into some sort of posthegemonic and postliberal trade regime.

About the Editor and Contributors

Gerard Curzon is professor at the Graduate Institute of International Studies and IMI Geneva.

Victoria Curzon Price is professor at the Graduate Institute for European Studies and IMI Geneva.

Meinhard Hilf is professor for international law at the University of Bielefeld, Federal Republic of Germany.

Hiroshi Kitamura is professor and former dean, Graduate School of International Relations, International University of Japan, Niigata, Japan; in 1988 Professor of International Economics, Department of Economics, University of Duisburg, Federal Republic of Germany.

Reinhard Rode is senior researcher at Peace Research Institute Frankfurt and lecturer at the Johann Wolfgang Goethe-Universität Frankfurt am Main, Federal Republic of Germany.

Jeffrey J. Schott is a former U.S. trade negotiator of the Tokyo Round and presently research fellow at the Institute for International Economics, Washington, D.C.

Bernhard Zepter is the deputy head of the delegation of the Federal Republic of Germany to the multilateral trade negotiations in Geneva and in this capacity negotiator in the Uruguay Round.